City Of Vain Dreamers

Lost In A Mirage

Pier Cefalo

Dedication

This book goes to all the kids that reside in our hearts and mind. I personally believe that there is a child inside all of us, even those that have lost track of themselves. This book is for all of them.

Acknowledgment

I would like to acknowledge everyone's efforts that went into the making of the book. My mind has been always a river of stories; maybe I daydream more than I should. But now when I look back on those times, I believe it's a good thing I kept most of those stories for my bedtime.

The reason why I kept those stories is because I felt I should try and tell some of them to the people around me. Of course, this one is a totally new story. It is not based on my childhood but on how the world behaves. It is the first time I have written a book. Thank you for reading it.

About the Author

Pier Cefalo is a web designer and developer, and this is his first book. He has been working on it for over a year. His family dates back to Italy, through Venezuela, and to the USA where he graduated. He can speak three languages and is trying to learn more.

Pier is starting his own company now but he has always been fond of unique stories. He has a love for mystery and unsolved things and he wants to find new ways to change the world without using violence, both of which are his motivation behind writing this book.

Preface

The City of Vain Dreamers charts the emotional, spiritual and intellectual journey of a regular schoolkid Kyle. Surrounded by vain, narcissist people, this young boy chooses to isolate himself from the external world. He observes the society around him and comes to see that selfishness, materialism and narcissism has permeated the lives and relationships of people.

Kyle has a mission: to help people understand that there is more to life than material possessions, and that there is more to living than being self-involved. And so, he embarks on a journey to enlighten people of the true value of human life. He is joined by his friends Jordan and Becca, who travel the same road by Kyle's side. The three tackle their world with its many challenges.

But then, they also encounter a new world....the one hidden behind the surface of a shining mirror, deep inside a forest glade. What is the new world all about? Are the people inside as conceited as the ones outside? Or is there a sinister force at work, trying to destroy humanity from within? Kyle and his companions are about to find out!

Contents

Page Left Blank Intentionally

Chapter 1 – I Am the Only One That Matters

Kyle heard indistinct voices as he sat quietly on his seat in the class. His hazel eyes were fixed on his sociology book, which had become a canvas of anime characters. Kyle liked painting and playing with colors, but he especially enjoyed drawing characters from his favorite anime. He sat there, scribbling on the paper, unaware of what was going on in the classroom. He gave little thought to what he was drawing and was more involved in thinking about the meaning of life – everyone thinks about that at some point in time.

Kyle was uncertain of what he wanted to do in the future and how his existence contributed to the improvement of this messed up world. He had chosen this hour of the day to think about the vast subject. Why was it necessary that he came into this world? Was he sent with a particular role to play or as an audience to watch others perform? Did he hold any significance in the hearts of the people around him? Could his sudden disappearance or non-existence bring any change around him or would the world still go about, ignoring the loss of a person like him?

Human life was so trivial and yet history was proof that even the smallest things in life could give birth to greatness. Could he be great enough to hide it beneath the surface of his achievements? He was busy contemplating the insignificance of his life and the whole concept of mattering to someone when he was suddenly interrupted by a loud bang on the table. *"Mr. Kyle Williams!"* shouted Mr. Gregory. His little bubble of imagination quickly burst, and his senses came back to life. His eyes shot right up at Mr. Gregory, who was standing in front of his seat, glaring down at him.

Mr. Gregory taught them mathematics. He was a short-heighted, plump man with spectacles that usually just sat on his nose while he gazed at the students from the top. Although he dressed up quite modestly, no one ever understood his queer obsession with flamingoes: he wore neckties of different colors with flamingoes all over them. He'd even put a pink flamingo keychain on his bag! Even though there were many odd, amusing things about Mr. Gregory, he petrified the children in school because of his strict, no-nonsense attitude. Kyle's eyes widened with fear, and without letting another moment pass, Mr. Gregory spoke loud and clear: *"Mr. Kyle Williams, this isn't your art class. Where is your math notebook?"* He pronounced each syllable clearly and put special emphasis on his name.

While Kyle was still processing everything, Mr. Gregory told him to leave the classroom. There was dead silence as Kyle started to travel his way from the seat to the classroom door. Hardly a minute had passed by when the school bell started ringing. A horde of kids came stampeding down the empty hallway. The school was over for the day, and Kyle had luckily escaped the punishment of standing outside the class. Yet, hearing the bell didn't change his mood much. He seemed indifferent to it and was still deeply engrossed in his thoughts.

Kyle was a fifteen-year-old kid who lived in a small house in Fountain Alley with his parents. Both his mom and dad worked late at night every day, and so he spent most of his time doing things on his own. He also had a little sister named Belle, who usually stayed with his grandparents. They lived a few miles away, but Kyle didn't particularly like going there because the children in that neighborhood bullied him. Kyle also had a speech impediment since he was born, which was the main reason why he was bullied a lot at school. As a result, he had become withdrawn from social settings and had started spending more time in his hideout watching Japanese anime cartoons on his tablet, and doodling pictures of them in his notebook. Kyle was also an avid reader and particularly liked classic literature; this was the subject he enjoyed the most out of all the others at school. He was a pretty good student overall, but lately, he had been drifting away from studies.

As he slowly walked towards home after school, he walked down the street, which was surrounded by huge oak trees. The thick, dense leaves made little way for the sunlight to peer through the leaves, throwing the street in shadows. His ash brown hair rustled like the leaves on the oak trees, and he kept walking with his gaze lowered.

"*K!*" a girl cried out from behind him. "*K!*" she shouted again. Kyle was named "*K*" when he was in the eighth grade, but it had been a while, and now people hardly remembered the nickname. This girl had a shrill voice that stopped Kyle in his tracks. He thought he recognized it. He turned around to see who it was. It was Marianne. She stood there in a blue floral dress, with her long dark hair tied up in a ponytail. She had an olive complexion which distinguished her from the other girls. There was no doubt that she was gorgeous. As a young girl, she was always the popular one, and even though Kyle tried to grab her attention, he failed to do so. She was really sweet to the people around her, but it was noticeable how she couldn't stop bragging about her possessions.

Her parents were quite wealthy but would hardly spend time with her. She wore branded clothes and went traveling during the summer holidays. Perhaps, this was the reason why she had gained much popularity among the kids. Kyle wasn't the least bit interested in how well-off she was; he just wanted to know her and be friends with her.

"Hey," said Kyle in a low voice. He seemed uninterested in striking any conversation at this time.

"Hey, K. How you doin'?"

"Fine, you?" said Kyle.

Without letting him answer his question, she hurriedly handed him a notebook and said, *"Look I'm in a bit of hurry, but here's Brianna's notebook, please return it to her when you come back to school tomorrow. I'm going on a trip to Japan for a week so I won't be here tomorrow."*

Another unintentional brag by Marianne. Kyle nodded his head and walked off. He looked at the notebook and turned to the first page of the book, which read *"Brianna Grace."* He wondered why Marianne had Brianna's notebook; she did have the habit of copying homework from other students so she could skip classes. With this thought in mind, he unzipped his bag and put the book inside. Kyle carried on with his casual stroll along the street.

His thoughts had occupied his mind so much that he forgot his way home. Instead of going through the road which he usually took, he turned left towards a narrow pathway which only had enough place to let bicycles pass through. Walking on the pavement, he started noticing the walls which had graffiti painted all over them. People's names were written all across them, which seemed like a minor attempt by the painters to achieve recognition.

Lately, Kyle had been thinking about his life and questioning the purpose of his existence. Although it was normal for such questions to arise in the minds of kids of Kyle's age, these paintings triggered rather grim thoughts that made him wonder about death and eternity. However, there was one more thought that was troubling him for a long time, and it related to narcissism. He had studied a lesson in his psychology class regarding narcissistic behavior and how ordinary people could secretly have narcissistic traits in them. He had grown up surrounded by narcissists – people who were inconsiderate and negative. When he thought about it, he found that even the few close people that he had possessed narcissist traits to some extent.

This thought brought back memories from the sixth grade, and he started to recollect his first encounter with a narcissist. It was his first day in the sixth grade when he met Jordan Nicholson. He was a curly-haired boy who had recently moved to Fountain Alley. The teacher made them sit together, and they would often do class assignments with each other's help.

As months passed by, they became quite close and spent the time after school playing video games together at Kyle's place. Even though Jordan Nicholson had quite a few friends, he was quite intelligent. Despite his intelligence, Jordan tended to criticize himself; Kyle would always point out his good attributes to cheer him up. After some time, Kyle noticed that he was the one complimenting Jordan on his achievements while Kyle's achievements went unnoticed or ignored. Soon after, Jordan slowly began to withdraw himself as soon as the final examinations came close. This was the time when Kyle needed Jordan, but he had stopped staying back with him, and hardly spoke to Kyle. After the examinations, Jordan found a new group of friends, and this shook Kyle's trust in friends for the first time.

It was after the first lesson about narcissists in the psychology class that Kyle realized how Jordan had used him. Jordan was a narcissist who always sought validation while he refused to reciprocate Kyle's friendship. He stayed with Kyle as long as he felt there was someone to cheer him up for his accomplishments. Then there came Marianne; the girl he liked in the seventh grade.

She was another person who displayed similar signs of narcissism in the way she boasted about her lavish lifestyle. She used to be surrounded by children and would be the teacher's favorite kid. Whether it was intentional or unintentional, Kyle did not intend to judge. However, these were the top two people on his secret list of narcissists that he had come across and for who he possibly developed an animosity. He had been taking notes in his head; it was as if he were going to conduct a survey to find out the characteristics that made up a narcissist. He knew another kind of narcissist that he grew up with. It was his father who was so obsessed with his accomplishments that he did not consider the value of what others person had achieved. Growing up, Kyle had two examples set before him; one was his dad who always let his mother down, and the other was his mother who wallowed in self-pity because there was no one around to share the pain with. Kyle was well aware of the relationship between his parents, but he had nothing to say in any matters of the house. Both of his parents worked till late at night, and he preferred this isolation over their bickering and quarrels when they were together at home.

While he saw narcissistic traits in his father that appeared in the form of his pride and tyrannical behavior towards his mother, he also noticed that his mother developed self-pity for herself – this, again, was another kind of narcissism. The graffiti on the wall also expanded his thoughts on this matter. Whoever the painters were, they had painted all over the walls with their names to display their creativity. Kyle thought deeply about this and questioned the narcissistic traits in people who so proudly exhibit their creativity through their artwork, music, or anything else that they make. It was kind of like they wanted to show off what they could do, perhaps in an attempt to use their talent as a channel to make their identity known. Kyle realized that it wasn't just the people closest to him who were narcissistic, but every human had a certain degree of narcissism running through their veins. Kyle even analyzed if this attribute showed up in relationships and friendships as well, to an extent. He understood that often, human beings only valued friendships because they had someone to love them and take care of them just the way they want themselves to be treated.

However, when the feelings didn't return, as was in the case of Jordan, they isolate themselves only to move on to someone who would feed their narcissism for a longer period. *"Perhaps,"* thought Kyle, *"we all were looking for friendships and love, not to love others selflessly but to gain the affection we think we deserve."*

At such a young age, Kyle was overthinking about matters that adults should be thinking about. His habit of spending time alone had made him an over-thinker over the years. Maybe these thoughts were conjured up by what the TV showed or maybe the psychology class which he attended left traces of itself in the corners of his mind. While some people had toxic narcissistic symptoms like his dad, some people subconsciously developed it as a result of what had taken place in their past. Marianne was an example of a person who found happiness in material things, and even though this seems totally narcissistic, there could be a possible reason why she turned to this person. It could be because her parents deprived her of their love and affection.

She took joy in what they bought for her, and she ended up going around bragging about her possessions. Similarly, his mother developed a sympathetic attitude towards herself, as no one genuinely understood her struggle. Kyle was an observant kid; he had started to believe that, although people looked vain and self-centered on the outside, they had a story hiding on the inside.

There was a reason for their behaviors. Kyle also realized that narcissism didn't have to be bad after all. It was inside of each one of us; it just needed to be tamed. It needed to be bridled to minimize the harmful effects on other people. Kyle also questioned why people thought that they were the only ones that mattered, and why other people's sufferings seemed to be trivial to them in comparison with their own problems? This pursuit of self-gratification was in vain, and people needed to become more empathetic. Kyle's heart ached at the folly of man. How he wished he could enlighten them with this illness called narcissism. It resided deep down in people's hearts, and they remained unaware of it. It was slowly spreading as people withdrew from each other and found solace in their own sense of grandiosity. While Kyle was deeply engrossed in his thoughts, he felt a heavy hand on his shoulder.

A shiver ran up his spine, and he stood there in astonishment. He couldn't move a limb out of fear. At this moment, he realized that he had taken the wrong way home. All kinds of negative possibilities started running through Kyle's mind; what if it was a gangster, or what if he had entered into a prohibited territory? He finally turned around and saw a tall man in shabby clothes, holding an empty bottle in his hand.

The man seemed to be drunk. Kyle mustered his courage and ran across the road. He kept running till he landed on the front porch of his house. It had been a rather adventurous day – that's how it always was in the world of his imagination. Kyle climbed up the stairs that led to his room and closed the door. His room had anime posters all over the walls, and books were lined up on the shelf. This was his secret hideout, which only Jordan was aware of; his parents already took very less interest in what he did in his life. Just above the ceiling, there was a glass window which showed the vast expanse of the sky if he lay down. He would often lie down there and fall deep into the world of his imagination where no one would interrupt him.

This was the place where he escaped into a world of the unusual that existed only in his mind. In his imagination, everything was perfect; people were happy, and evil did not exist. Here, people sought happiness in each other's company, could look through each other's hearts and recognize beauty. He had a dream to turn this unusual vision into reality, and he strongly believed that one day, his dream would come true.

Chapter 2 – One plus One Equals One?

A loud bang on the door, awakened Kyle. Engrossed in his imagination of a perfectly happy world, he had fallen into a deep sleep. He heard another bang as he squinted in the dark. He had not switched on the lights when he came into his room that afternoon because there was sufficient light shining through the glass window on the ceiling. However, it had become very dark now, which indicated that he had been sleeping for a long time. Squinting and tripping, he opened the door.

"Kyle, baby, is everything okay? Why are the lights switched off?" asked Kyle's mother.

Mrs. Williams was a pretty and tall woman, with brown curls that fell down to her shoulders. She had thin arms and large hands. There was a permanent crease between her raised eyebrows, right in the middle of her forehead, indicating signs of perpetual stress. She looked tired as she had just returned from work, but today, she had taken time off work earlier than usual. She rushed into the room and switched the lights on.

"Kyle, baby, say something. I'm worried about you. I know I hardly get time to spend with you and..."

"Mom, I'm fine. Trust me, I'm fine. I just fell asleep and forgot to turn on the lights," said Kyle, still rubbing his eyes and trying to retrieve his consciousness.

He was a little surprised at what his mother had said to him.

Worried? About me? What *else, she wants to spend time with me* now?

Kyle's parents did not have a healthy relationship with each other. They usually fought whenever they were together, and this troubled Kyle. However, his mother loved him a lot, and despite her being busy through the day, she still wanted to connect with him because he was all that she had.

Belle used to stay with her grandparents, and even though Mrs. Williams wanted to develop a mother-daughter bond with her, she knew that bringing Belle back home would only make her feel deprived, much like Kyle. All the things that Kyle had experienced made him hold a grudge against his parents, and no matter how much they displayed affection on an individual level, Kyle's mind remained fixed on their relationship. The thought that troubled him was how he could never be with them like other kids were with their parents. Kyle was pretty surprised at this sudden revelation that had seemingly dawned on his mother concerning his solitude. He laughed and mocked the thought of it in his head. It brought a sarcastic smile on his face.

"Well, I'm glad to hear that, Mom. Thanks," said Kyle.

"Honey, wash your face and come downstairs. I've prepared dinner for us. Your dad isn't here, so it's just the two of us," said Mrs. Williams. Picking up the empty packet of chips and throwing it in the little dustbin, she hurried down the stairs.

Kyle shut the door that his mother had left open. He turned back and looked at himself in the mirror. *Mirror! What a great way to boost up your narcissism!* He thought to himself. He rolled his eyes and went to the bathroom, splashed water on his face, came out, dried his face with a towel, and walked down the stairs. He was famished after a long day of adventure and only just realized that he had not eaten anything after his meager breakfast in the morning and his body felt weak. He came and sat on the table while his mother served him. Kyle was quite shocked at the sudden change in his mother's behavior, yet he liked the care which seemed out of the ordinary to him. The house seemed calm with a slightly dull vibe. He was still feeling groggy, so he poured himself a glass of chilled water.

Mrs. Williams had made turkey bacon sandwiches and mashed potatoes which Kyle absolutely loved. Right now, however, he seemed rather unimpressed by it. Yet, he smiled at his mother while she looked at him with an anticipation of a compliment.

Kyle smiled and took the first bite. *"It's good. Thanks,"* he said.

"How was your day, honey?" asked Mrs. Williams.

"Huh?"

"Your day. How was your day at school?" inquired Mrs. Williams with eyes that looked tired but also happy.

"Oh, yeah. It was fine," said Kyle, smiling back.

"How was your mathematics class?" asked Mrs. Williams.

"Um…" Kyle raised his eyebrows in astonishment. He had forgotten the incident with Mr. Gregory in the morning. He still had mashed potatoes in his mouth and chewed with his mouth stuffed while grinning embarrassingly. Then his mood changed again. He became serious as he suspected that his mother might have received the news from school. Finishing the morsel in his mouth, he said, *"Um, it was good, Mom."*

"Listen, Kyle," Mrs. Williams began. Her expressions had transformed, as well. She seemed like she was about to scold him, but at the same time, she looked concerned. She knew that her relationship with her husband and the resultant loneliness in Kyle's life was affecting him – and not in a good way. She knew she was responsible, and this became another reason for her to pity herself for being incapable of taking care of her son's physical and mental health.

"Mr. Gregory called in the evening. He told me that you don't pay attention in class. You also failed in your mathematics test. Honey, you know that you can talk to me about your thoughts. What's troubling you, dear?" asked Mrs. Williams.

Kyle looked straight at her with a softened gaze. He felt as if it had been ages that someone wished to know what he felt. Everybody he knew had been so self-centered and interested in their own lives that no one bothered to ask him even a simple question like that. Among those self-centered people were his parents as well. However, now it was his mother who had asked this question. At that moment, he felt bliss. He did not say anything, nor did he pick up his spoon to resume eating. He just spent that brief moment staring at his mother with admiration and respect. Evidently, there was no source of comfort better than feeling heard.

"*Say something, Kyle,*" said Mrs. Williams.

As usual, Kyle's thoughts took over him, but this time, the thoughts were related to the present situation.

"*Mom, I love you. Thanks for asking,*" replied, Kyle.

Even though many things were going on in his head, this little set of words made their way out of his lips; Kyle could not express what he had in his head; he was just grateful and surprised at the same time. He smiled, got up from his chair, and planted a kiss on his mom's cheek. Then she walked up the stairs back to his hideout.

Mrs. Williams was expecting an answer and seemed a little disappointed at not getting one. However, she finished her plate and got up to clean the table. Upstairs, Kyle was on his bed with a notebook and pen. He was busy with his hobby of drawing anime characters while simultaneously contemplating life. He thought about what had happened at the dinner table. A sense of peace entered his thought process. He thought of how little kindness shown to a person could boost up a person's mood; words had this insane ability to tear people down, but at the same time, they had the power to build people up, too. He had just experienced the power of words.

His mother, a narcissist, in his opinion, had displayed kindness that he had been craving. He also realized that he had undoubtedly been misunderstanding her. While the world was mistreating him, his mother had actually loved him sincerely. After his birth, she had left her studies in fine arts and started working. She wanted to build a future for Kyle, and he and Belle were the only reason that she was working so hard. Was this a sign that narcissism was curable? If yes, then what was the antidote to it? What could bring about this massive change? Whatever it was, he did understand that people could be changed; they only needed someone to help them. They only needed a hand to pull them out of the abyss. Just like there was a certain percentage of narcissism in people, so was there a certain amount of love. All it needed was someone to discover it and bring it out. Kyle believed he could be that hand. He could help people by encouraging them to interact with each other. According to him, all that was needed was the seed of empathy to be planted. Yes, empathy was the cure for narcissism. He felt like the appointed task was especially for him. A sudden rush of adrenaline flowed through his body as he felt like a superhero.

He decided to play games and activities with people to create this sense of empathy and to eliminate narcissism. Kyle wanted people to be kind, to value other people's happiness above theirs, and always to be mindful of the struggles that a person next to them must be going through. The little act of compassion by his mother had kindled a fire in him to redeem humanity and save them from this fatal disease. He was all set for this mission now. With this thought in mind, he shut his eyes and slipped into his imagination once again. He knew he would soon be able to make his dreams come true. The next day, he woke up earlier than usual to have breakfast with his parents. He had developed a habit to wake up late and make his own breakfast so that he could avoid his parents' company at the very start of the day. However, this day, he woke up, took a bath, got dressed, and ran downstairs. His mom and dad were sitting at the table. He was a little late for breakfast. As soon as he took his chair at the table, his parents looked at each other with surprise. They seemed genuinely happy to see him make an appearance at the breakfast table.

He quickly grabbed a bowl and poured cereal and milk into it, and acted as if there was nothing to be shocked about. He saw how his parents had been quiet all this while; they simply sat there to finish their food so they could leave soon after that. Noticing the echoing silence on the table, he decided to strike up a conversation with them.

"Um, Dad, how are you? It's been a while since I have spoken to you. How is work?" Kyle asked. He sounded very formal as if he were conducting an interview session with his father.

"I'm fine, champ. Work has become a little hectic, but it's all good. How are you?" said Mr. Williams.

"I'm great, Dad. Mom made amazing dinner yesterday – turkey bacon sandwiches and mashed potatoes. They were absolutely delicious. Wish you were there, too," Kyle answered.

Mrs. Williams gave an embarrassed grin. It had been years since Mr. William had complimented her and Kyle mentioning how delicious the food was had created an atmosphere of awkwardness.

"Oh, really? You didn't leave some for me, Lily?" said Mr. Williams. Lily was Mrs. Williams' first name.

"I did think of it, but then I thought you might have already dined out," replied Mrs. Williams.

Both of Kyle's parents were talking now, and he felt this contentment in his heart. He longed to see them care for each other, and for himself have a normal life like the other kids at school. He felt if that happened, he would finally be free of his troubling thoughts and would enjoy some time with them as other kids do with their parents.

"It's no surprise, Lily, that you have always had the habit of making assumptions in your head," mocked Mr. Williams.

"I thought that because you usually do have dinner with your office colleagues," said Mrs. Williams.

"Yes, because I find some interesting company there unlike home."

Kyle looked at both of them and listened to this sarcastic exchange of comments. Mr. Williams had picked up a negative element from Mrs. Williams' statement.

"You are never going to understand me!" Mrs. Williams complained loudly and stormed out of the room.

That was a quick change in her behavior, Kyle observed. So much hatred had been breeding in his parents' minds that they could not listen to each other with patience. He looked at his dad with angry eyes; he was busy having his breakfast, unbothered at having upset his wife. Mr. Williams finished his plate, grabbed his car keys, and left for work while Kyle sat there, trying to comprehend what had just happened.

This was his first attempt to make his parents interact, but he had ended up getting a negative response. Nevertheless, he picked up his bag and thought of leaving. To Kyle, it seemed that creating empathy in his parent's minds would be difficult because they were older, and it had taken years for them to turn into these narcissistic beings that they had become. The mere thought of it saddened him but decided to push the feeling away as he left for school. He was running late. Entering his school, Kyle saw Marianne and Brianna having a conversation. He went close to them and said, 'hi.' Both the girls smiled back at him. Kyle returned Brianna's book, and she left before he could strike up a conversation.

Kyle was left alone with Marianne, and they began walking towards their math class in complete silence. After a while, Kyle started making jokes on his messed-up hair and how odd he looked in a red polo. He also spoke to Marianne about how these things did not matter – what mattered was being kind to people. Marianne listened to him quietly.

"Hey, may I sit with you today?" asked Kyle. Marianne nodded, and quickly sat next to Kyle as Mr. Gregory entered the classroom.

Mr. Gregory glanced across the classroom and heaved a sigh. *"All right, class. I have checked all your test papers, and today, I'm going to reveal the results."*

The students sat there in anticipation. Kyle, too, was anxious and feared his doom. He already knew that he had failed in the mathematics test. Toward the end of the class, Mr. Gregory began calling out names.

"Sarah, Matthew, Jake, Marianne..." These were the names of the people who had passed the test.

Mr. Gregory called out all the names of the people. The only one left was Kyle. Suddenly, everybody looked at him as if he was from outer space and did not belong to the same specie as them. He felt as if he would either be abandoned or imprisoned for committing this horrendous crime of flunking his math test.

"Stand up, Mr. Kyle Williams," said Mr. Gregory. *"Nice polo shirt."* All the children started giggling at how weird he looked. *"Are you planning to be a cartoonist one day because all I find you doing lately is creating sketches of yourself while we are studying mathematics,"* said Mr. Gregory.

"Those are anime characters, sir," whispered Kyle. Another wave of laughter went around the classroom.

"Anime? Well, Mr. Kyle, you come to school for a purpose. I want you to pay attention during the class or stay at home drawing those stupid cartoons. Do you

understand?" Mr. Gregory stated in a stern voice.

For the past few days, Kyle had not been in a normal state of mind, which was why he failed to concentrate in class. Anyway, the bell rang, and the children got up, all gossiping and laughing about how he had become the subject of a joke. Kyle walked out of the classroom, embarrassed as his self-esteem shattered into pieces. They failed to see what he was going through; he lacked love and affection, and his disturbed life meant he had problems concentrating. Here he was, trying to build people up, but he saw how it had little effect on them. Everyone lacked empathy and did not care about the emotions of others. Children or elders, all had become hardened and numb to other people's feelings.

It seemed like narcissism was all over the face of the earth, and curing, it was impossible. As he walked about the street, he looked at the number of homeless people who were lined up at the corner of the lanes. They were alone in their misery, and nobody offered to help them. Some of them were handicapped, and this explained why they were unable to work and get off the streets. Kyle was deeply moved as he saw the pain in their eyes. There was no empathy in people's hearts, and this withheld them from helping such people who were so badly in need of help. There was this massive barrier among people that they failed to break through. They could not understand or feel, and for a while, Kyle felt like he could not save humanity from this disease anymore. He felt frustrated that he could not do anything. Perhaps he was too young or too weak, or the world was not for him. Agony and humiliation burned him to the core of his existence as he walked back home.

Chapter 3 – Between Worlds

Standing on the front porch of his house, Kyle heard footsteps rushing towards him. It was Jordan Nicholson who was struggling to catch his breath. It seemed like he had been running for a while now to match Kyle's pace. Kyle turned around and glanced away out of embarrassment of what had happened in the math class earlier today. Kyle had worn his black cardigan on the way home to hide his red polo shirt, despite the scorching heat in the afternoon.

He was almost sweating as he stood there, waiting to unlock the door and hide in his little cave of imagination. Kyle had already gone through a lot. Now, with utter hopelessness in humanity and extreme humiliation that he had experienced, he could no longer stand anyone's presence. He sensed betrayal in everyone's eyes and their tones. He did not want to read into what people said, and believe that everyone was good at heart. Kyle was a superhero that had returned defeated, unable to conquer the enormous giant that was slowly devouring the city.

He stood there, waiting for Jordan to speak up. He did not have enough courage to invite further disgrace. His eyes looked strained, perhaps due to the sunny weather or maybe because of the weight of the thoughts on his mind. Jordan immediately recognized the black cardigan that Kyle was wearing. Mrs. Williams had bought two similar-looking cardigans on Christmas for Jordan and Kyle. The one that belonged to Jordan still lay somewhere in the corner of his closet. After their friendship had come to an end, Jordan had put away everything that reminded him of Kyle.

However, it seemed like Kyle had not been able to get rid of them, neither the things nor the memories. Jordan felt a hint of remorse as he saw the cardigan, and the old memories kicked in. In that brief moment of silence, where Kyle waited for Jordan to speak up, Jordan was somewhat overwhelmed with emotions. He regretted his cruel behavior towards his one true friend. Over the years, he had failed to find a friend as genuine and considerate as Kyle.

Suddenly, without realizing Jordan said, "Hey, that cardigan. It's the coolest thing I ever got as a present. Man, I miss those days. I still have mine. It's been years that I have not worn it, though."

Kyle looked at Jordan with suspicion.

"Is Mrs. Williams at home?"

He began to peer through the window with mild excitement until he looked at the grim look on Kyle's face.

He stood straight and said, *"I'm sorry, I just... I'm sorry about what happened at school today."*

Kyle shook his head in dismay. All this while, Kyle was observing Jordan very calculatedly. He doubted Jordan's intentions and wanted to know what he was truly up to.

Kyle thought to himself, *"Is he here to rub salt into my wounds and to further aggravate my pain? Is he delighted to see the cardigan, or is he making fun of how I was wearing it in this hot weather? Why is he even concerned in the first place? Had he forgotten what he did to me, was it not enough to tear someone down and distort their view of friendship for the rest of their life?"*

"Why are you here?" Kyle whispered.

Confused, Jordan squinted at his face as if he knew that Kyle would repeat himself to make it clear.

"I'm asking, why are you here? What do you want after everything that has happened?" he spoke a little loudly this time.

"Please leave; I do not wish to inflict more insult upon myself."

Although Kyle spoke sternly to display the firmness in his decision, his voice quivered. He was almost on the verge of a mental breakdown, but he did not wish to express himself in front of Jordan.

"I just came to ask you if you are okay. Why aren't you focusing on your studies lately?" Jordan asked.

"I'm okay. Please leave me alone," said Kyle.

"Uh, also, I have two tickets for the concert at the fairground. I would really like if you come along," asked Jordan with a slight tone of friendliness in an attempt to ignore the statement that Kyle had just uttered.

"I said, please leave me alone," Kyle replied in a louder and harsh manner to Jordan's invitation.

Kyle was clearly beaten down today. Although no one really knew his internal struggles and his quest to redeem humanity, at least Jordan could tell something was up, and he was genuinely concerned. At Kyle's continued resistance and unwillingness to interact with anyone, Jordan bid him farewell and left. Kyle opened the door and went inside where his mother waited to welcome him. This seemed unusual because he did not expect a welcome after a long hard day at school, and today had been the worst. In all honesty, Kyle felt no comfort in finding his mom at home. Rather, he felt this uneasiness and anger remembering what had taken place in the morning. He did not want to be comforted by anyone because everyone had failed in understanding him.

"Mom, please. I do not want to talk about anything," Kyle blurted out.

His voice was shaky, and his eyes welled up. *"Leave me alone!"* He quickly ran up the stairs while Mrs. Williams stood there, watching him in perplexity. She loved her son, and it was hard for her to see him distressed. After all, she was his mother and was making attempts to establish a strong mother and son relationship. However, she failed to see that it was too late. Isolation had marked the days of Kyle's life until today – and now, his mother had suddenly entered into his little world and started displaying affection, so it was a bit of a surprise to him. The actions of all the people around him sounded like disguised mockery. He felt that the people were only showing love because they secretly wanted something from him, but Kyle was tired now. He just wanted to spend some time alone, because that's where he didn't feel the need of explaining himself or experience any disappointment.

Kyle entered his room, threw the cardigan on the floor, and tossed off his shoes. He laid on the bed as an act of surrender. He was utterly frustrated. While his heart and mind refused to be comforted, his body felt too weak to bear any weight. He was upset at the things that he had been dealing with; narcissism was an epidemic that was slowly overtaking the world, and nobody was noticing it, let alone doing anything about it.

There was no empathy in the world anymore. People were only concerned with what they felt, what they needed, and what they lacked. They only prioritized themselves. There was an absence of love and kindness, and all you could find outside were people walking around with masks on their faces. They hid from others and also did not wish to see the reality of other people's personalities. It was a plastic world with plastic people who only dedicated their attention to clothing and materialistic things instead of real people. There was anger, hatred, and inconsideration towards the pain of others. Kyle lay on his bed, staring at the sky through the ceiling window. Birds flew around freely through the blue expanse. They were flying with careless ease, not worrying about what could happen to them.

The sky was limitless, and the birds knew they belonged to them. It was home, and there was freedom. Why could he not experience this freedom of expression in his world? Why was there fear lurking around and anxiety to bug him constantly? Why is it that all he could find was judgment and labels imposed on him when he stepped out? Was there no kind heart in this little city where he lived?

People had become monsters. No one could blame them for who knew the reasons why they were a certain way? However, they could certainly be held accountable for how they were treating others. Every one experiences good and bad days in life. Bad might even be an understatement, but holding the same behavior towards others would never really end cruelty. One has to stop at one point and turn around to face his past. They have to command the bad side of them to stop controlling them. The war was not in the world outside, but it was within, and every person had to take up a sword and slay that giant of ego and selfishness. Today's incidence had acted as a fuel to ignite the fury inside Kyle. All the years of emotional build-up had finally taken its toll. On this day, Kyle gave up his decision to bring a change. It seemed impossible because it was not his work.

Apparently, he was the only one who cared, but he could not change others. Everyone had the power to change themselves, which eventually helped them change the world. It was a collective work, and he could not do it on his own. Kyle closed his eyes. He felt a slow calm settling in his bones, and suddenly, he felt at peace. It was similar to the calm one feels after a storm subsides.

Looking at the sky did have that effect on him; it cleared his head of negativity. When he glanced into the sky, he knew that the world was not limited to the ground beneath. There was more to it. There was something unknown that was yet to be discovered by him, and this gave him a sense of tranquility. Right now, he closed his eyes and imagined the same sky, but now in his head. How wide and clear the expanse seemed! His eyelids became heavy, and he began slipping into another world in his head. This world was perfect, and not in terms of mundane things like fancy clothes, elaborate furniture, and expensive cars which usually surrounded him. This was an ideal world because it had a unique sense of peace, joy, and freedom – all that he had been unable to experience in his own life. Here, beauty had a whole new definition, and peace had not become extinct.

This peace was not false, it was not derived from temporary pleasures and vain pursuits. It was serenity, unlike the world outside. Kyle imagined a little boy playing in a field of wheat with the parents cheering and calling him to themselves. The mother held a baby in her arms. The boy ran into the field after a butterfly he happened to see. The butterfly went farther, and he followed.

Kyle could recognize the parents as his own, so it was apparent that, perhaps, the little kid was himself and the little baby was his sister. He recollected that the picture in his head was from his childhood memories. It dated back to the time when his family was living in a village with his grandparents, and he was around three years old at that time.

Life as a child seemed perfect and free from stress and negativity. Although the snares of the world still encompassed him, he was immune to it. Kyle had embraced everything that life brought to him with an open heart. Who knew at that stage of innocence that the world would unveil itself as a hideous monster? Who had the slightest idea that childhood was the first and the last time where he could taste freedom and pure joy? Who had thought that the future would be a parched land where rivers of peace would not flow?

Basically, the perfect world that he had imagined all along was something he had already experienced once before. For how could anyone crave sweet without tasting it? There are things in our lives that we long for so desperately, because somewhere along the journey, we have been touched by it, like the whiff of fragrance that brushes past you on winter evenings. You have a picture embedded in your head; otherwise, you would not even know that something like it exists. For instance, as children, we only come to know what's bad for us when our parents set a standard for us. We learn to differentiate between right and wrong.

But before the imparting of knowledge, we do not view the world through the filter placed on our eyes. Similarly, in our relationships, we tend to expect more from people because we have been treated in a better way previously or we look at other relationships that portray perfection which we do not see in our relationships. Our expectations basically stem from a place where we see the potential in something which may not come from the current state of affairs. Kyle was engrossed in the thoughts of all the things that his heart wanted, from affection to peace.

In his thoughts, he imagined a happy relationship between his parents, a strong friendship with Jordan, a world with people who have a love for each other, and where everyone was sensitive to the each other's pain. He imagined a place where he could do everything he wanted to do and where there would be no boundaries to stop him.

In such a world, he would make sure to eradicate all narcissism and self-centeredness. The only center of his universe would be to maintain a healthy environment that focuses not just on physical health, but mental health as well. He knew the importance of a healthy mind as he was a victim of depression and anxiety. In his world, there would be no sign of a mental disorder or any physical or emotional pain. People would be mindful of each other and would work for each other's welfare. Material things would not hold any importance in their heart, and they would keep themselves connected to nature to find tranquility. The chirping sound of the birds soothed Kyle's ears as he lay there in peace. The stress of school and the negativity in his head had receded like the ocean tides.

This was the home where he belonged, where he had freedom like the birds, where he flew in the limitless sky with nothing tying him down to the ground. Suddenly, Kyle felt a tug at his feet. He looked down and what he saw left him astonished. There were numerous people – even some with unrecognizable faces staring up at him.

He was trying to soar into the sky and fly away, but these people grabbed his feet with such intensity that he was unable to escape. He heard voices that he could not recognize. He shrugged his feet with all his might. As he did that, the people let go of him, but he flew away without any control over his body. He felt like he was a helium balloon, soaring upwards uncontrollably. However, the farther he went, the more sadness he felt in his heart.

He felt like he was leaving a part of him on the ground, something that added value and purpose to him. The sky, even though it was beautiful, contained nothing but emptiness, and up there, he was on his own. There was no one there, only more loneliness. He looked down and only saw people looking up at him as if they hoped that he would come down and rescue them.

Kyle flew in the sky but found nothing that could satisfy him. He did try coming down, but he failed to do so; there was no way back. With the weight of sadness on his heart, he immediately opened his eyes and realized that he had slipped into a deep sleep while pondering over his perfect world. He woke up in a pool of sweat, shaking from fear at what he had seen.

The dream felt so real that he still felt the pain in his feet. In his brief vision, he sensed what eternal detachment would feel like. The voices and the faces seemed real, too. What did they mean exactly? Was there something that his subconscious mind was indicating to him? Whatever it was, he woke up even more troubled than he was before.

Chapter 4 – The Heart That Rules

The dream had shaken Kyle's existence. The sadness and unusual emotions that he felt still lingered, and he felt a deep sense of uneasiness. He woke up feeling out of place and absolutely petrified. The dream had such an effect on him because it did not seem very different from reality and because he remembered every detail of it as vividly as if it had actually taken place.

It seemed like a mysterious spiritual awakening or perhaps it was the universe's attempt to remind Kyle of his purpose. Whatever it was, he had to examine it. He knew that brushing it off would not be so easy, and the discomfort might still badger his conscience like guilt. Yes, that was the closest explanation to what he was feeling: guilt.

The only thing was that it was not guilt – and if it was guilt, then what was his crime? Kyle looked at the clock; it was dinner time. He immediately gathered his emotions and decided to go downstairs. Before that, however, he rushed into the bathroom to take a quick bath. The anxiety induced by the dream had left him sweating and shaking. Also, his face clearly displayed the fear though it had subsided a little by now. Kyle let the water fall on his body, and he felt the heat rise off his skin. Perhaps he had developed a fever because of the traumatic experience, but he did not want his mother to suspect it. He stepped out of the bathroom and put on his comfy clothes. He was still a little warm, but his appearance did not show any particular signs of illness or stress. He walked down the stairs and found his mother setting up the table.

The room was dimly lit, and the patter of raindrops falling on the window sill could be heard very clearly. It had been raining heavily outside, but he had not noticed this after waking up. His thoughts were so occupied by the dream he'd had that he had failed to notice the things around him. He came and sat on the chair while his mother was still busy with food preparation. The cold wind entering through an open window had made it very chilly inside, and Kyle shivered a little. The whiff of food coming through the kitchen infused some vigor in his weak limbs. The long tiring day, the fever, and the cold weather outside necessitated a nice, warm meal.

Mrs. William served Kyle some rice, and he sighed at the mere sight of it. They both ate the food in silence, only exchanging smiles every now and then. The silence lengthened, but it was no uncomfortable. When they were finished eating, Mrs. William smiled and said, *"It's raining here after such a long time. Fountain Alley hardly gets any rain – doesn't that totally contradict its name?"*

Kyle sat there, listening to her. The food had filled him up, and he felt much better.

"I remember, it was three years ago that it rained last. We were coming back from Grandma's when our car broke down in the stormy weather. A man who lived close by helped us out, and we finally made it home. Even today, that moment of panic and helplessness does not go away when I think about rain," said Mrs. Williams, looking out into the dark from the window.

Rain in Fountain Alley had not been a blessing for the residents. The rainy days were always an awful experience for the people of this city, and therefore, it seldom pleased them when they heard about rain. But then there were a few days when the floodgates of heaven showered upon this city without bringing any harm – and today was one such day.

Kyle and his mother sat on the couch, eating soup, and enjoying the serenity inside the house. He thought of how the state of his mind was exactly opposite to the reality of his life. For instance, the outside realm was peaceful and calm while the inside of his brain was chaotic; in contrast, the current situation was that it was comfortable and peaceful inside but stormy outside. Kyle did realize the importance of having peace within. Any outward tranquility was futile if the heart was always troubled by disturbing thoughts. He had experienced this deeply, and he knew that in such situations, every attempt of seeking comfort outside of oneself is in vain.

"Kyle, I know that there is something that has been troubling you lately," Mrs. Williams said in a low, affectionate tone. Her voice had a typical motherly concern in it. *"I really don't know what it is, and it is fine if you do not want to share. But I want you to know one thing..."*

Kyle looked at her in anticipation. He wondered what she was about to say. Was it something bad? Was she going to tell him to correct the way he had been acting lately? Kyle's anxiety worsened by the second. Mrs. Williams could sense it as she saw him staring at her with his eyes wide open.

"Relax Kyle; I'm not going to scold you," she said gently. *"I just wanted to give you a piece of advice that I want you to remember for the rest of your life."*

"The mind is a messed-up place. It is a place with porous walls which easily allows worry to enter and destroy your character. You see, your mind is the only pathway for troubles to affect you. However, your heart is the one place which requires a lot of time to let anything enter it. It is guarded and safe, and it's the heart where you must safeguard your peace. You have two choices to live by: live by what your mind tells you, or what your heart tells you. The wise man always follows his heart because he knows that his mind is influenced by the world, but the heart holds the essence of his character."

Kyle blinked, attentively listening to and absorbing these profound words of wisdom.

His mother continued, *"I have made the mistake of never listening to my heart. I learned the importance of it eventually, but I really wish someone would have taught this to me when I was young."* She sighed, staring at him with unseeing eyes. The rain outside had eased off, and the loud thunderous noise was no longer audible. For that brief moment, they both enjoyed the silence…while it lasted. A sharp knock on the door broke the stillness in the room. Mrs. Williams got up to see who it was. It was Mr. Williams who had decided to come home early from work because his office had an electricity breakdown. *"It was useless staying at work,"* he said, shrugging out of his coat.

As soon as Kyle heard his father's voice, he quietly got up and walked stealthily up the stairs that were at the back of the door so his father could not see him. Kyle wanted the wise words of his mother to settle deep inside his heart. He wanted to spend some time in solitude to ponder over all she had said to him. He knew that staying downstairs might just affect him negatively; he was sick already and couldn't bear more negative things. So he quietly walked up the stairs.

Kyle entered the room and closed the door behind him. Quietly, he lay down on the bed. He could feel pain in his limbs as his body rested against the soft mattress. He began to think about what his mother had told him and knew exactly what she meant when she told him to follow his heart. He had spent all his time being driven by his mind which, in turn, had only been fed by the lies of the world. He had not listened to his heart.

However, Kyle also understood that the heart was nothing without the mind. If the heart was the chariot, then the mind was the horse, and he needed to learn to bridle it. The heart was largely affected and influenced by the mind. Now, he found himself trapped in the paradox where he was told to follow his heart, but he realized that if he did that, it would not be very different from what the world had been doing.

The mind and the heart must be granted equal power. If dominance is given to just any one of them, then it may just tear down a person completely. Kyle was considering all this in the light of narcissism, but his mother had a completely different purpose of saying it. She did not want Kyle to be so affected by the world at such a young age. She knew that a lifetime of worry and overthinking amounted to nothing, and what a person really needed was peace in their hearts.

This piece of wisdom did seem like a biased statement, but it was not. It was more like a defense mechanism to deal with the mind's vile thoughts, and Kyle needed it – at least to some extent. In the very least, he needed to balance out the power between his heart and mind. After much contemplation about the matter of the heart and mind, Kyle slipped into a deep sleep.

This was one conflict that many philosophers had spent their entire lives talking about. It was a mystery that could never fully be solved. There was no other way but to accept it just the way it was, and Kyle was too young to think that this mystery had a solution. That night, Kyle had the same dream again, but this time, it was clearer than before. This time, however, he knew that it was a dream and not reality. Kyle saw himself up in the sky, moving upwards; he saw the same people tugging at his feet, but this time, he could see more familiar faces. There was his mom, dad, Marianne, Jordan, and many other faces that he could not identify by name.

It seemed like they were calling out to him, screaming in desperation, but he could not hear what they were saying; he was going higher and higher in the sky. When he glanced upwards, he saw that the sky was endless, and he did not go up into space. He soared so high that the clouds blurred his view, and he could not even see the people on the ground. The emptiness was emotionally gripping and, just like before, he felt a strange gloominess envelop him. He felt he had no sense of purpose here. He did not know where he was heading; he was lonely and detached from the people who were yearning for him to come back to the ground, and no matter how much he attempted to go back, he could not. Even though Kyle was dreaming, he felt tears trickle from his eyes - the dream was that intensely melancholic. There was nothing up there, and Kyle was now trapped in this place. In the agonizing helplessness, he began to cry out loudly. He knew that no one could possibly hear him, but he kept crying. Suddenly, he broke free from whatever was lifting him up, and he found himself falling swiftly from the sky. He was high above in the clouds, and he screamed as gravity pulled him back down.

Kyle shot straight up as his dream ended. He did not find himself tumbling to the ground but back in his bed in the real world. His face was wet with sweat and tears. His heart was beating so fast, it was as if he had really experienced a free fall. He rubbed his arms, shivering with anxiety. Kyle tried to calm himself down and let the feelings recede. Yet, he could not let go of the dream; it kept playing in his head on a loop. This time, he was sure that it was not a coincidence but an awakening, and he felt that his dream did make sense, but he needed to learn something more about it. Kyle got up and began to pace to and fro trying, to align all his chaotic thoughts. He felt like he was the chosen one who was appointed for a purpose by the universe. However, he had been failing to distinguish between things so far; but now, he was sifting through his thoughts so he could come in contact with his real identity. His dream held a meaning; it was a reflection of what he had been doing in reality.

He had been consistently keeping himself protected and detached from people because of their behavior toward him. His failure in eradicating narcissism had only made him more defensive. He even failed to see his mother's love and affection because he was so absorbed by his paranoia. In his dreams, he was soaring into the sky; in reality, he was drifting away from the people who cared about him the most.

His city needed him; it was a city of vain dreamers, materialism, and narcissism. Absence of empathy fuelled this city, and he was the one who could go out and help people instead of running away from things. Running away was a sign of cowardice, and it would only cause him more loneliness and melancholy. No man was an island. Everyone needed to be found, understood, loved, and cared for. He did not deserve solitude, and neither did the people deserve to be ignored.

While solitude was reassuring and comforting, it could make a person a victim of their mental musings. Kyle had finally come to this realization. He decided to stand his ground. He was born with a purpose which was being a person who would benefit everyone. Isolation could not fulfill his purpose. He knew, sooner or later, he would have to face his fear.

Chapter 5 – Opening the Gate

The next morning, Kyle woke up as the alarm blared right beside his bed. His mother's words still resounded in his ears. The ambiance of tranquility and the enlightenment caused by the revelation of his purpose had helped him sleep soundly through the night. His body still ached as he forced himself out of bed, but he felt rested enough to be active through the day ahead. He walked into the bathroom, took off his clothes, and turned on the shower. The cold water refreshed and revived him. He quickly toweled off, got dressed, and exited his room with his backpack.

Kyle decided to take the bus instead of walking. There wasn't enough time, so he had to skip breakfast. Kyle usually walked to school because he wanted to avoid any interaction with the children on his bus at all costs. He did not like taking the bus because a few months back, some of the kids on the bus had bullied him. A boy named Jake and a bunch of other boys, who were a part of Jake's circle had made fun of the way Kyle spoke and how he dressed up. One day, they even dumped spaghetti on his clothes, and Kyle had to go back home to clean it up. He could not handle the embarrassment daily, so he preferred the other option, which was to walk to school. However, today, Kyle felt the urge to dispel his fears and take a courageous step. He had developed a fearless attitude as he realized that there were many things to fear in life, and little kids of the same age group taunting and making fun of him was probably the last thing he should be worried about. What one actually needed to dread was the loss of relationships, friendships, and death, which was the ultimate bridge that you would cross.

A dying conscience, poisoned by the bitterness of life, tainted human beings' inner ability to differentiate between good and evil. The bus stopped, and Kyle gave a sweeping glance through the seats as children stared right into his face. He chose to sit in the backseat right beside Becca in a vain attempt to avoid confrontation of any sort with Jake and his squad. Becca was a pink-haired girl from his class, a literature nerd like him. She was probably even a bigger nerd than him. She was quite famous for completing the 100-books-a-month challenge. Yes, that sounds unrealistic, but Becca's ability to read faster than the other kids did give her an upper hand.

She had read almost every classic literature novel and would often quote exact dialogues, leaving everyone astounded. Not only could she read very fast, but she could also memorize quicker and better than an average kid. She was a gifted child, as most teachers often said. Becca had her nose buried in a book, and when she saw Kyle sitting right next to her, she gave him a keen glance but did not ask any questions. Perhaps her literary wisdom had compelled her to not make any inquiries in the presence of the evil squad. She continued reading, and Kyle diverted his attention to the world outside the window of the bus.

All heads in the bus turned every now and then to look at Kyle sitting in the backseat. He heard whispers, but Kyle had no intention to pay attention to them. He did not want to feed his mind with negativity right at the start of the day. He almost felt like a celebrity, the kids gave him so much attention; however, he had never particularly desired to be in the spotlight. He was the kind of person who would wear an invisibility cloak for the rest of his life if he could. However, this fine morning, he wanted to step out of his comfort zone and do what he should have done earlier. He wanted to interact with people, listen to them, and be heard by them.

He wanted to leave behind the life of isolation he had lived so far. Thus, he ignored what was going on in front of him and observed the pedestrians on the street instead. The roads still glistened because of last night's heavy rain, and the people walked along the pavements to avoid stepping into the puddles. The water had settled on the road in small pools. This is what usually happened in Fountain Alley after each spell of rain. The water would settle in the roads, standing there for days to come. In some cases, water would fill the streets to the point that it would inch up to the knees of the pedestrians. Kyle felt grateful for the choice he had made though it came with a price, as all choices do.

Kyle knew that after spending so much time seeking an escape from reality and running away from people, it was going to be immensely challenging to build bridges and remove the barriers. Communication had already been hard for him, but it was time to open the gate and allow people into his life. He needed to demolish the wall he had constructed over time just as much as he needed to break the barriers of narcissism that people had created. He wanted to bring a change, and he was starting with himself. Also, Kyle knew full well that changing people would not happen overnight, and he had to take down the wall brick by brick. Doing this and extricating people from this plague of narcissism required assistance and support. Kyle realized that the only way to be different and to make the difference simultaneously was to try and make his friends be a part of his new world. He decided to talk to his friend Jordan, share the idea with him, and see what he thought about it. Jordan's display of concern after the humiliation Kyle had faced in the classroom had really altered his image in Kyle's mind.

Deep down, they both loved each other, but they could not muster the courage to express their affection to one another. Both of them could not be blamed for such an attitude as mankind had always struggled with choosing honesty and vulnerability, even when relationships were at stake. After all that had happened in the past, Jordan was very hesitant to reunite with Kyle, but the last incident allowed him a bit of courage to take a step forward. Kyle had also undergone an inner revival that had changed his mindset. He had experienced a moment of awakening and wanted to transmit the same awakening to all the people around him.

Finally, Kyle was willing to take the first step and let go of grudges. He knew that Jordan was the person who had extended his hand in friendship to him. It was time that he, too, forgot the past and relied on the support of his long lost friend to accomplish his ultimate goal of curing narcissism.

Kyle reached school and began walking towards the hallway. He could spot Jordan from far off. He weaved through the swarm of children and grabbed the chance to strike a conversation with Jordan as soon as he was within hearing.

"Hey," said Kyle. He was struggling to catch his breath, but he smiled anyway. *"What's up, bro?"*

"Not much," said Jordan, holding a stack of books in his hand. *"Mrs. Kelly just handed me these notebooks, so I have to keep these in the classroom."*

Mrs. Kelly was their psychology teacher who was loved by all her students. She was a cancer survivor with a prosthetic leg, so she needed assistance in carrying her stuff. She was an elderly woman who was an inspiration to a lot of students because of her exemplary teaching skills. Jordan was one of the helpful kids who were always ready to help her. Her method of teaching sometimes combined psychology with biblical aspects, and truth be told, she did make the students ponder deeply about life and its complexities. Kyle was one of those students whose lives she had impacted; he admitted that part of his ability to think deeply stemmed from Mrs. Kelly's teachings.

Jordan put the books on the table, and he and Kyle sat on the same bench. Other students were still entering the classroom and taking their seats. In the middle of the laughter and chatter of the students, no one would pay attention to their conversation.

"How was the concert?" asked Kyle.

"Oh, it was great! I wished you were there too," said Jordan.

"I'm sorry for being so rude to you that day. I was going through so much that I did not wish to interact with anyone," Kyle apologized.

"It's all right. I understand, mate," said Jordan.

Kyle smiled affectionately at Jordan who continued, *"I apologize for what I did to you earlier. I have always been waiting for the right time to express my feelings, but I guess there is no such thing as the right time. All we got is right here and now."*

Kyle had not expected this, but he was glad that Jordan was finally speaking his heart out. He said, *"It's okay. Everyone makes mistakes, but what's more important is the realization that should follow."*

"Yes!" exclaimed Jordan as he stretched his hand to give Kyle a high-five.

Kyle high-fived back, and Jordan said, *"I missed you, Kyle Williams."*

Kyle giggled and said, *"I missed you too, Jordan Nicholson."*

Everyone turned silent as Mrs. Kelly entered the classroom.

"Okay, children. Enough of the hullabaloo. Please be seated," she said loudly.

All the children rushed to their seats, and Mrs. Kelly began to write on the whiteboard with a blue marker. She wrote, *"Ecclesiastes 4:9-12."*

All the children knew that it was a reference from the Bible, but very few actually knew what it said. Kyle was one of the many who had no idea what it was about.

"Two are better than one because they have a good return for their labor: If either of them falls down, one can help the other up. But pity anyone who falls and has no one to help them up. Also, if two lay down together, they will keep warm. But how can one keep warm alone? Though one may be overpowered, two can defend themselves. A cord of three strands cannot break easily." In the end, she underlined, *"A cord of three strands cannot break easily."*

All the children read the verse out loud as Mrs. Kelly wrote down every word on the whiteboard.

"Now, I have an assignment for all of you that you have to work on in teams. The purpose of this verse is to make you understand the importance and impact of strong relationships, and how the outcome is very different from when you are working alone. You have to run a survey and do some research regarding this topic. By the next class, the project details will be given to all of you. Until then, you can divide yourselves into pairs," Mrs. Kelly explained.

This was one of the many examples of biblical theology that Mrs. Kelly had applied to psychological studies to increase impact and comprehension. The children quickly changed seats and chose a partner for themselves. Jordan and Kyle did not need to hurry as they had each other's back. The class was over. Kyle marveled at the Bible verse that he had never read before. He was too young, and the only religious knowledge that he had acquired was from school. However, he felt like the verse had spoken to him in particular.

Only today, he had realized the importance of interacting and connecting with people instead of living in isolation – and the very same day, the class lecture had covered the same topic. It didn't seem like a coincidence to him. Kyle was slowly accepting it was better to have people with you because they extend support and can help each other through thick and thin.

Kyle had already decided to make Jordan his partner. He had also resolved to spread the message of the dire need of eliminating narcissism. The verse he read in the class only strengthened his decision. The city of vain dreamers did not require a superhero. It required a team that was willing to collectively and devotedly work towards one mission. It was the kind of world where the only way to survive was by working together as a group. With this realization, Kyle invited Jordan to stay over at his place as it was a Friday. Tonight, he would unveil his master plan to redeem his people.

Chapter 6 – Take Me There

"Whoa! Bro, that's unfair! That was clearly a fluke!" cried Jordan as Kyle's chest puffed up like a valiant soldier.

The two had been playing on the play station for a while now, and Kyle had won twelve games in a row. Jordan sat down on the couch with his face buried in his hands as Kyle joyously jumped up and down, celebrating his victory.

"Bro, admit your defeat. Admit it!" said Kyle as he laughed hysterically at Jordan's futile attempts to beat him.

"The thing is that it's been a while since I played games and I'm out of practice," said Jordan.

"Oh, really?" Kyle replied, and the two giggled.

It had certainly been a long time since they sat together to play video games and enjoy each other's company. As they played, they reminisced about the good old days. They were talking and munching on nachos while they shot each other in the game.

"Okay, bro. So, let's get down to some real talk," said Kyle as Jordan listened intently.

"I told you earlier about my thoughts, right? About life and narcissism and how I wish to bring about a change? I want to invite you to help me in my cause."

"You're talking like we're about to devise a plan to conquer the world," said Jordan with an excited grin on his face.

"Close enough," smiled Kyle.

"I know the plan may seem a little foolish, but I think that we can actually compel people to analyze themselves and to awaken their dead consciences. Life's been harsh already, and if we can do something to diminish the casualties, what can be better than that?"

Jordan straightened his face as he carefully analyzed every word that Kyle said.

"You know narcissism has dug its claws in our society. Our society is filled with materialism, and I am tired. I am tired of this vainness, and I'm tired of seeing this false happiness in people's eyes that they find in their selfish ambitions.

"The people closest to us are struggling with it, but they are ignorant of the root cause. They have no idea what they

have made of themselves and how their selfishness is impacting the people around them."

As Kyle spoke, it reminded Jordan of what he had done in the past; he lowered his gaze as he ruminated over how he had contributed to this wave of evil as well.

"Bro, are you listening?" Kyle demanded an answer.

Jordan nodded and smiled.

"So, yeah. Are you with me on this?"

"Of course, I'm with you and always will be," replied Jordan.

It was a moment of unifying strength for Kyle as he realized the power of love and friendships. Their friendship was one like David and Jonathan in the Bible story – they had a perfect bond where they were ready to support each other through life's challenges. This time, Jordan did not want to disappoint Kyle and Kyle had open-heartedly forgiven Jordan for what happened in the past.

Kyle switched on his laptop and logged on to *Squid,* which was an online messaging app that one of the school's ex-student had created. That kid was a computer geek who had created numerous apps and games online which had gained much recognition in the school campus. He was a victim of bullying, and *'squid'* was actually the name kids called him. He used this name as a slap on his bullies faces. While they flunked in their exams, he had used his creativity for a beneficial purpose. *Squid* was a success as all the children at Kyle's school used it to interact with each other.

There were various chat rooms and conference calls that you could easily join on *Squid*. Many teachers sent notes online during exams, and students would talk to each other frequently using the instant messenger. Even though *Squid* was a safe platform to hold interactions, cyberbullying was still taking place. This was why Kyle had tried to keep away from the app, too. He seldom used it for interacting, and when he did use it, it was solely for studies.

However, Kyle now realized the importance of it and typed in a message: *'Hello. Do you think there is a greater purpose that you are born for? If you wish to use your unique talent for the greater good, then attend a free and secret meet up at 12 Avenue, Fountain Alley, after school hours. See you there.'*

Kyle typed in the message and showed it to Jordan. Jordan added to the text, '*Psst. Free ice-cream.*'

"*Now, they'll come,*" said Jordan as they both laughed and pressed 'send,' forwarding the message to all the kids in their class.

Kyle felt anxious as a few minutes passed.

"*I don't know, man. I suddenly don't feel good,*" he said.

"*Relax. Everything is going to be all right. Don't worry,* " said Jordan, patting Kyle's back.

The next Monday, Kyle entered the school hallway and looked around. There were fifteen more minutes to go until the school bell rang. He saw that there were strange expressions on everyone's face. He saw the kids whispering as they stood by their lockers, pretending to take out books but really sharing their thoughts about last day's text message.

Kyle exchanged a glance with Jordan as they met in the hallway. Brianna, too, had received the message. She seemed the kind of person who would not come to the meeting; so did many kids who seemed to be uninterested and unimpressed by the bait that Kyle and Jordan had thrown. It sure seemed like an evil plan because of their clever strategy to lure people in, but they had their eyes fixed on the goal which was to collectively work to achieve a happy and loving society free from narcissism and materialism. The school bell rang, and the children rushed into the class. Jordan and Kyle both felt anxious now as the clock hands moved. The whole day, the school's environment was different, especially in the cafeteria. Children were curious to know what the message was about, but they were hesitant to share, hoping they were the only lucky winners of this opportunity to use their talents to the fullest. The message was certainly not a lie. Every word was true, but it was concealed and condensed.

The kids would have to use their talents before they could take part in the great purpose. And the ice-cream? Well, that was not a false promise either. Jordan's uncle had an ice-cream parlor from where they had already ordered enough ice-cream cones to give away. In a nutshell, all the things stated in the message were true, but it was the suspense they had created that persuaded the kids to come and find out what the message was all about. And so, as the last class ended and everyone walked down the hallway, some headed home while others stayed behind to visit 12 Avenue, Fountain Alley. Jordan stood beside the letter post close to Kyle's house. As the children came by, they were directed toward the garage of Kyle's house. The garage was empty as his parents were not home; there was enough space to seat 30 children. There were white plastic chairs aligned in perfect order. As the children entered, they chose their favorite spot and sat down in anticipation of the commencement of the meeting. Slowly all chairs were filled, and Jordan entered into the garage. He closed the door behind him. The garage was properly cleaned, and it seemed like a lot of effort was put into fixing the place.

There was a whiteboard right in front of the chairs; Kyle stood next to it, looking as though he was about to teach a lesson to the present students, and share his wisdom with them. The silence in the garage made the creaking sound of an old rocking chair in the corner quite audible. The garage was more like a storeroom, so his parents cared little about what Kyle was usually doing there. Kyle would play games or just sit quietly drawing sketches so he could easily use this place for his meeting. Kyle and Jordan looked at the children of their classroom. They were all familiar faces, some of which seemed embarrassed because they had not shared with their friends in school that they were attending this meeting. Then others looked intrigued. They all looked forward to the meeting. Kyle began his speech; the one he thought would bring about a revival that no preacher or revolutionist had been able to bring. He was putting forward an idea that could change the course of the world, and change the standards of modern society. It seemed like a meeting of rebels who aimed to overthrow the evil kingdom that was ruling over them. He stood there as Moses, ready to lead the Israelites out of the land of slavery, but this slavery was to narcissism.

"Good evening. I appreciate your cooperation and support to come and take part in this campaign. If you are here today, it means that you received the text that was sent to you. That suggests that you already know what you have been called for and that you desire to use your talents and abilities for a greater cause."

The children listened attentively to his elaborate speech.

"Fellow student," Kyle continued his speech, *"We all have been gifted with various talents, and we do desire to do something great, but what if we achieve this greatness together?"*

71

The students all looked confused, yet they continued listening intently to Kyle, who wrote on the whiteboard: '*Narcissism.*' He resumed speaking: *"I'm sure you all are familiar with this term. The other words for narcissism would be selfishness or self-centeredness, which is something that is embedded in our society. Materialism, hate, and our inability to love each other are woven into our daily lives. We find there is little room to accommodate our old values and morals. Today, I invite you to use your great talents and make a change around the world. Do little things for each other, love one another, and spread happiness."*

The children's faces displayed perplexity.

"Do you disagree with the society, Kyle?" said Brianna rolling her eyes.

Some guys at the back said, *"Oh, so you're starting a new movement now?"*

A burst of laughter was heard as Kyle's face fell with dismay.

Tom, a boy in a row farther back, said, *"Kyle, is this a part of the assignment Mrs. Kelly gave?"*

"Get a life, boys. You guys definitely don't have anything

else to do," said Cindy.

The speech went over the children's heads. Some of them listened quietly whereas others bombarded Kyle and Jordan with sarcastic remarks. Jordan tried to pacify them and keep them seated, but an uproar started as the boys in the back row hooted loudly. These kids considered Kyle's idea utterly foolish because of their failure to understand what he was saying; other kids did understand, yet they thought it was a boring idea that would yield no results. After constant attempts to convince the children, Kyle became silent. It was yet another disappointing situation. Slowly, the children left the garage.

The creak of the garage door echoed loudly as all the children marched out in unison towards their respective homes. Kyle and Jordan felt helpless as if they had made a joke out of themselves. Was their strategy incorrect? But they had not even explained the whole plan yet. Was the audience wrong? If such young children were difficult to influence, then changing the whole society was a dream.

"Was the goal too foolish to be achieved?" they settled down in discouragement and self-doubt.

The ice-cream lay in the refrigerator, and the hearts of the children remained cold. The meet up was an epic failure, so they packed up the stuff, switched off the lights, and headed towards Kyle's room. Kyle entered the room and switched on the lights. They both sat on the couch. Kyle offered Jordan a cup of coffee, and they both ordered sandwiches and ate. Things had not turned out as they had planned and, once again, everything was a mess. For Jordan, it was the first incidence of disappointment, but for Kyle, this behavior had become quite constant. However, they still found joy in each other's company.

Kyle turned on the play station, and they became engrossed in virtual reality – a place where things were in control, and the bad guys could be shot, while the good guys spread joy. How easy it was to switch between players and look at the world anew, unlike the real world! Despite everything, there was a silver lining: Kyle had company now. He was not alone with his thoughts and could share them with someone who had the same mindset as him. The sound of gunshots from the TV was the only thing that could be heard. After a while, they heard a knock on the door. Following the second knock, Kyle turned down the volume and opened the door of his room. It was Becca. She had rung the bell, asking for Kyle's notes. Mrs. Williams had suggested that she go to his room and ask him for it directly. Kyle and Jordan were confused, and Becca stood at the door.

"Oh, come in, Becca." Kyle invited her in after realizing that they had been staring at her in silence for quite some time.

Becca sat on the couch next to Jordan and glanced at the entire room. She seemed quite impressed by the books on the shelves and the anime posters. Becca was one of the girls who did not interact much, and that is why they did not know each other. At present, Becca was marveling at the art and books in Kyle's room while Jordan and Kyle, still confused, waited for an explanation from her.

"Um, Kyle. I thought much about what you said today. I know you both are shocked to see me, but I am not here to contribute to the humiliation."

They both stayed quiet.

"I would like to join you both in this quest."

Kyle and Jordan were astounded that there was another person who was willing to help. So, the meeting was not that bad, after all! At least, it had successfully convinced Becca to take part in their plan. Kyle's face brightened up, and Jordan grinned as Becca uttered those words. And so, Kyle found himself with two friends, Jordan and Becca, who pledged to make his dream come true. Becca, Kyle, and Jordan sat and discussed the idea, and Becca shared her thoughts on the subject as well.

Becca was born to a wealthy family where the pursuit of materialism was encouraged. Her dad was an architect, and the owner of many houses. Becca took little interest in his money and would always ask for love and attention from him, while he encouraged her to be like him. Becca was a gifted kid, but it seemed like her parents were planning to use her more like an asset to make them proud, especially in social gatherings.

She was like one of them; a victim of narcissism, but her conscience was alive. She knew the importance of love, friendship, and family, and wished to demolish all societal standards. This was the first meeting the three of them had with each other. While Jordan and Kyle's friendship was already unbreakable, they felt having Becca by their side was an added blessing.

Days passed, and Jordan and Becca religiously met at Kyle's house. It was not just Kyle's hideout anymore but theirs too. It was a place where they shared their thoughts, ideas, problems, and played together. They opened up to each other about their internal battles, their struggles, and their dreams. In addition to that, they had adventures there; they explored places and made memories. Nevertheless, in every situation, they held each other up like the cord of the three strands that couldn't break easily.

Mrs. Kelly taught more to them on the lesson from the Bible, and they valued learning the concepts in each other's presence. They were the odd ones out – the ones who retaliated against societies' rules and wished to finish narcissism. They believed that if not today, then someday surely narcissism will be removed from the earth and it would be a happy, peaceful, and safe place to live in. Someday, things would be more apparent as all bad memories would blur away, and people will develop empathy for each other. They cared deeply for the world. They were with like-minded and shared the same goal now. It was a blessing for them to have found each other.

Chapter 7 – Look at Yourself through a Mirror

Three months had passed since the fateful day of the meeting. During this time, Becca's friendship with Kyle and Jordan had only grown stronger. When they hung out together, the worries of the world did not bother them much. They had found a form of escape in each other's company. They understood each other and were always present to listen to one another's problems. It was not like they never fought; they had their disagreements, as normal teenagers do, but what was different was that they were always willing to resolve those fights, and find a way out of their troubles together.

With many things in common as well as their many differences, they always showed an accepting attitude towards each other. At school, this unlikely trio received much opposition and was made the butt of all jokes. It became especially worse when the news of Becca's strong support for Kyle and Jordan spread through the classrooms. The children bashed her and even stopped appreciating her talents and intelligence, which they earlier considered as her best quality. People wrote harsh remarks on the trio's benches and often left notes in their bags or at their doorsteps criticizing their little initiative to make the world a better place. *Squid* was the most common medium that the haters used as a shotgun, as they never had the guts to confront the three of them directly. Anonymous texts and inbox messages were sent to them until they deactivated their accounts and closed the door to all the negativity. This struggle with hate lasted all through the three months; now, finally tired, the children had reduced their hateful acts to only gazes of contempt.

This experience had left these Kyle, Jordan, and Becca stronger than before. Their friendship deepened, and so did their belief that narcissism and materialism were unacceptable. As Kyle's room and garage became their usual spot to hang out, they explored their way to the forest located right behind his house. On one of the days, when it was drizzling, they stepped out of the window of the attic and sat on the brick roofs. Kyle's parents were not home, and even if they were, no one really cared about his safety anyway. On this day, the three friends sat on the slope of the roof and talked till evening fell.

They could see the sun setting on top of the giant forest trees. Becca, feeling too adventurous, began walking farther down the slope to the branch of the tree that rested on the corner of the roof. The two stopped her, but she beckoned them to join her. She stepped onto the branch, slightly scared, but very excited to climb the tree. She was quite athletic in school as well and was always open to trying new things. She held the branches tightly, and with small steps, climbed down to the ground.

The tree was quite tall, and its branches were too strong to break, so she gripped onto it like a monkey and disappeared into the leaves. Kyle and Jordan were thrilled and curious and decided to follow her. Kyle struggled a little, but finally, his feet touched the ground. They were amazed at the beautiful forest glades.

The chirping of the birds was quite clear, and Kyle wondered why he had not dared to come here before. It was a great place to play, they decided. They could climb trees, play hide and seek, and explore new plants and animals in the wild. Since then, the forest became another place where they would play if they were not in the mood to sit back at home and play video games.

They feared the parents more than they feared any wild animal, so as soon as the sun would set, they would climb up and go back to the room through the attic window. Later, they even placed a ladder at the tree to make their regular climb up and down easier. Fences guarded the leafy paradise that the three had discovered; that is why there was no other way to enter other than using the roof. They enjoyed spending their time here in nature and in each other's company. The trees were like skyscrapers touching the sky. The place looked especially beautiful when they stood on the mossy ground and looked up at the clouds through the cover of leaves. The one rare thing was that birds of various kinds lived in the trees.

There were only a few high rises and skyscrapers around the city. This was another sad truth; Fountain Alley did not have a lot of tall buildings, but Kyle had seen the city life on his visits to New York with his dad. He could not find any trees there, but all he could see were colossal giants of cement which were home to a vast population of people. Society had swept away any traces of nature as their hearts, too, had hardened like cement. One part of the problem was a consequence of the disconnection with nature; society had created a barrier between itself and the nature that God had created. This had influenced them to become so engrossed in their own daily chores that they failed to see the beauty in the surroundings. As a result, they had become insensitive to each other's sentiments as well.

"You may win every time we play car racing on the play station, Kyle, but I'm a fast runner than you," said Jordan as he hit Kyle and ran ahead of him. Becca sat there, reading one of her books based on survival in the wilds. They had set large stones on the ground where they sat. It was the forest glade where trees were not as dense as they were in the rest of the woods. They often walked around exploring, but never dared going forward as they feared losing their way back home.

However, at the moment, Jordan and Kyle forgot all caution and both went running behind the trees and the snapping branches. They stepped into the little puddles of water at the roots of trees and dodged the barriers that came in their way. Their laughter echoed in the woods, accompanied by the sweet humming of the birds. Meanwhile, Becca sat there, uninterested in what they were doing, totally absorbed in the interesting book she was reading. The three friends had been planning to stay in the forest for a week to experience what survival truly is like. They were inspired by a show on television that recorded all the experiences of one man who had decided to make videos as he taught methods and strategies to cope with life's real challenges and giving the viewers a clear picture of what it was like before society forsook nature. Becca was reading about the same topic and underlining important points while also noting them down in her notebooks. Besides this one book, she had twenty more books at home that she had collected over the years that she intended to learn from.

Jordan came running towards where Becca was sitting. Laughing and panting after hours of running, he finally sat on the stone next to her and wiped the sweat off his face. His clothes were all drenched in sweat, and he could not say anything except breathe heavily. Becca threw an annoyed look at him and buried her nose back into the book. *"Where's Kyle?"* she asked, her gaze still fixed on the letters in the book.

"He hid somewhere, I guess. I was too tired, so I came back here. I called out his name a few times, but he didn't answer, so I returned here."

"Oh," Becca said.

"Yeah," Jordan nodded, *"I know Kyle is hiding from me. He'll just come back once he is tired, too."*

Jordan picked up Becca's notebook and busied himself reading the notes she had taken down. They kept themselves busy talking about the various plants that were edible and would come in handy as they tried surviving in the wild, and also the other plants that they should avoid at all costs.

Kyle had no inkling of what Becca and Jordan were up to. He had walked deeper into the forest, exploring the places they had not seen yet. He was playing with Jordan, but the beauty around him was a big distraction. As Jordan's voice faded, Kyle did not care to answer or to go back to him. He kept walking, every now and then stirred by the slightest sound coming from the trees. The leaves were wet, and there was a little place to walk between the canopy of trees.

Kyle's shoes were covered with dirt as he had accidentally stepped too deep into the sludge. The further he walked, the more intrigued he became to find out what lay ahead, hidden among the dense flora. He saw signs carved on the trees, and juice cans in the corner which were showing signs that the forest, after all, was not an undiscovered place. Some people had come here at some point perhaps to camp, or to investigate, or maybe to practice survival. If not that, then there must be some other reason; what was confirmed was that this place had been discovered by humans already. Kyle kept walking ahead, not willing to turn back. His interest peaked as he found new items; everything he saw stirred his imagination. He even stumbled upon a child's shoe which seemed worn out; that told him that the little children who had played here had done so a long time ago. Maybe this fence was built later. Perhaps he was not even born at that time. These little things he saw prompted his speculations, and he was fascinated. He imagined all kinds of stories that may lie behind everything.

As Kyle proceeded, he accidentally stepped into a pool of quicksand. He fell on his back, while his left foot remained stuck in the gooey mud. He jerked his foot back, which he was able to extract from the slush successfully; however, his shoe came off and remained stuck in the sand. When he pulled out his foot, he dragged himself backward and suddenly hit what felt like a hard, heavy wall. The thud of his body and the pain that shot through his arm startled him.

For a moment, he hesitated to turn his head and see what was behind him. Slowly, though, Kyle turned his head around. He wanted to see what exactly was there he had come up against. To his surprise, he saw a big mirror. It seemed to be a part of a dressing table. Moss and dirt covered it, and the leaves were woven through its frame as if they grew, making their way up.

A few visible patches of the mirror reflected Kyle's image back to him; the rest of the mirror did not show a thing because it was so dirty. Kyle decided to walk away. He took a step back and thought that it was the right decision to end his exploration right here, and maybe revisit the spot some other day to find out what it was and why it was here. Also, after coming this far, he suddenly realized that Jordan and Becca might be looking for him.

Now, there lay a choice before him: to clear the mirror and stay here for a while or to go back and maybe come some other day with both his friends. Therefore, without even glancing properly in the mirror, he turned around to walk. That's when a loud creak came from behind him. Kyle quickly hid behind the nearest tree, trying to find refuge in these fortresses and hide away from any anticipated danger.

After a few seconds, Kyle realized it was just a squirrel that had climbed up a bent branch of the tree. He stopped, turned, and began to inspect the mirror. He decided to stay for a little while longer, hoping that Jordan and Becca would come looking for him if something significant arose. It was a cloudy afternoon, and they had enough time to stay there before the sunset. Kyle stepped forward to clean the dirt; finding nothing else, he took off his T-shirt. He wiped off the dirt and stood in front of it, marveling not on his own appearance or the strangeness of humans, but on how the mirror was the most narcissistic object that could ever exist. He had never thought about this before, but at present, nature surrounded him and offered him more beautiful things to watch than his own image.

Kyle realized that the mirror was just a vain object that only showed a superficial picture, always failing to capture what was within. A mirror could capture every wrinkle, every scar. It could reflect the image just as it was. It could fill a human being's heart with pride, or point out their insecurities to such an extent that the person would not want to look in the mirror again. However, with all this blatant honesty, the mirror failed to show a picture of what lay inside the human heart. It never showed what the outer skin concealed; it never revealed the beauty hiding behind physical ugliness. Mirror was a protagonist in this story of narcissism; it accentuated the materialistic parts without letting anybody know how quickly one's appearance can perish. It failed to show that if a person is stripped off their physical form, all that remained was a picture which was very different from what they could see in the mirror. Yet, mirrors were considered an essential item of need by society. They glorified the mirror as the only mode of measuring one's self-worth.

Kyle was lost in his thoughts when he noticed that there were rays of light emitting from the mirror. At first, he thought that light was peering in through the leaves and causing this effect, but it was a dumb idea as the light was very strange and completely different from the rays of sunlight. Kyle was perplexed at this sight and feared to touch the mirror. He didn't want to be jolted by an accidental current! He called out loudly, *"Becca! Jordan!"* Even after calling out their names a few times, he did not hear a single reply. Again, he turned around and cupped his hands around his mouth to make his voice sound sharper and louder.

"Jordan! Becca!" The air carried around the echoes of his voice and dispersed slowly. Kyle had come much too far in the woods for his voice to reach both of his friends. At the same time, Becca and Jordan, who were still in the forest glade, wondered where Kyle was. Becca began to think of all the possible positive reasons while Jordan rushed towards the denser parts of the woods to locate Kyle. On one side, Kyle shouted their names, while on the other, they looked for him, crying out loud.

After waiting for a response, Kyle accepted the silence, pushed aside his fear, and decided to look closer at the mirror. It looked like energy was passing through it. Unafraid, he leaned forward and placed his hand on the surface to feel the energy and examine the source of light.

To his astonishment, his hand passed right through the glass. He freaked out and quickly pulled it back. His eyes widened with shock, and he stood absolutely motionless. He even forgot to breathe as his mind tried to make sense of the strangeness that had just occurred. What was it? Kyle was now curious to find out if it was reality or a dream. He rubbed his eyes and pinched himself, thinking he was in a dream.

He put his hand through the mirror again, and his entire arm went through it. He could feel no trace of pain in his arm, and so he passed his other arm through the surface as well. Eventually, he walked straight into the mirror. What lay ahead of him inside the mirror boggled his mind. Kyle stumbled back out of utter shock. Was this some kind of portal, a doorway to another world? He retreated without any second thoughts. Kyle entered into another forest on the other side, which was not very different from what he had come out of. He turned around, and the mirror was still there, but this time, its back was towards him.

His body was the same, and he had a certainty that he was not dead; it felt like anything but death! He observed that even though he had entered through a similar-looking mirror, the forest was very different on this side from the one he had come from. There was a path in front of him where there were no trees. It was a clear path that led towards another trail. Kyle could not comprehend what was happening. How could it possibly be true that there was another world somewhere? Was it a portal to a parallel universe? His thoughts skipped and jumped, as though at the speed of light, as he tried to make sense of the events taking place before him. He had to find out where he was and needed to tell Jordan and Becca about this.

Chapter 8 – Abyss of Dimensions

Kyle had made his way into an unknown world. He was gripped with fear and amazement as he tried to analyze what had taken place. For a moment, the memories of himself as a kid, his parents, and Jordan and Becca flashed in front of his eyes. It was as if they were the only people who had a place in his life. In those moments, he thought of them as he if were dying, but then he shrugged the thoughts away and tried to recover from the grasp of his emotions. The mirror certainly did not have any effect on his body, but his mind ached with perplexity.

Kyle had a feeling that he was leaving something very precious behind. Although he knew that the mirror was the portal to his way back home, his anxiety compelled him to believe that he may never return, that he would forever be stuck in this abyss. The astonishment had paralyzed his legs, and even though he wished to move forward, his fears did not allow him to act. Finally, he rekindled his courage and took a few steps, taking small strides and being very cautious of any strange movements around him.

This place could be dangerous, but his curiosity still overpowered his fears. The wild surrounded him, and he could hear the rustling of the trees. Encompassed by dense trees, plants, and canopied by leaves, he could not figure out if it was afternoon or evening. The pathway in the middle of the forest was still clear enough to suggest a way that he could follow. Kyle knew that this was the path that he needed to trace so he could explore what lay at the end of this road. As he inched his way forward, he suddenly heard a loud growl from behind the trees towards his left. He stopped dead in his tracks.

Another growl followed the first one, and Kyle scrambled back towards the mirror. He had walked quite a distance from it. Upon moving, he saw that the mirror looked exactly what it looked like on the other side – only here, it was cleaner, and there were no plants woven through the frame. It seemed as if someone cleaned it regularly. He heard another growl, and this time, it was louder than before. He sprinted towards the mirror and ran straight across, coming back to the real world. He had no idea where the growl came from or what the creature was, but he knew that whatever it was, it had seen him and it had growled at him.

Now, as he ran straight through the mirror into the real world, he stumbled and fell face down into the mud again. On the other side from where he came, there was a puddle – and he had tumbled right into it! He struggled to get up and out of the swamp. As he got on his feet, he heard Becca and Jordan shouting in the distance.

Looking for Kyle, Becca and Jordan had come far into the woods. They were close to the place where the mirror was. When Kyle heard them, he picked up a stone and threw it in the direction of the trees from where their voices rose. Mud covered Kyle's face, and he was still so petrified by the experience that his mouth refused to move. He threw another stone, and it hit Becca who was standing behind the leaves.

"Ouch, what was that?" she said.

She pushed aside the thick blanket of leaves, which was the only thing that was separating them now. Becca saw Kyle and ran to help him. Jordan came running after her and found Kyle in a dazed state. Becca became very worried because they had been looking for him for so long. They had looked behind every tree and had come so far in search of him. There was no doubt that they all loved each other dearly, and they could not even think of losing one another.

Her face was tense, and she quickly grabbed a bottle of water from her backpack and splashed it on Kyle's face. Jordan's reaction was very different; he burst out laughing when he saw Kyle because he remembered how they were playing with each other earlier. Becca gave him a serious look as if to quiet him down with her stare alone. She did have that power in her eyes. Her gaze was quite intimidating for other kids at school, even though most of the time, she was a polite person. She extracted Kyle from the mud, and Jordan's laughter disappeared on being the recipient of Becca's deathly stare. He, too, bent forward to help Kyle.

"What happened, buddy? Where were you?" he asked out of genuine concern.

"We have been looking for you for so long..." Becca began, looking at Kyle with a frown on her face.

They both kept asking him such questions, expecting that he would answer, but Kyle stared at their faces without saying a word.

"How did you end up here?" Jordan asked.

Kyle's lips quivered as he tried to speak. Jordan offered him water to drink. As he gulped down the water, he began to regain his strength. The paralysis also seemed to leave his body, and he sighed deeply as the jaws of death released him. Becca and Jordan breathed a sigh of relief to see Kyle recover. He had turned pale earlier as he tried to speak, but now he looked better than before. Becca and Jordan were focused on Kyle, and they didn't even look at the mirror behind him. They were too worried to pay attention to the trivial things around them. *"Kyle, buddy, say something,"* insisted Jordan.

"S-s-something v-very s-strange happened," Kyle stuttered.

"What?" inquired Becca.

"There is another world just like this one. That mirror over there is the portal that leads to it," he said, pointing towards the mirror that was leaning against the huge oak tree.

Kyle quickly got up on his feet and said, *"I'm not kidding, guys. This mirror, right here, is not an ordinary mirror. There is a world that lies inside of this glass."*

Jordan and Becca exchanged glances as they heard Kyle's unbelievable story.

"Um, Kyle, relax. This is a normal effect of falling on your head. It will be okay," said Becca, thinking that maybe a concussion was the cause of his strange hallucinations.

Jordan patted his back as a form of sympathy, but Kyle shrugged his shoulders and said, *"Guys, I'm not lying. There's a world through this mirror where I tried to go. There is a forest on the other side with a pathway that leads to* someplace, *but I could not explore because a loud growl from an animal* on *the other side of the forest frightened me."*

The same convincing and robust power of his speech that had successfully persuaded Becca to be a part of their group now convinced both Jordan and Becca to believe him.

"Well, clearly the way he shivers shows something was seriously wrong with him," Becca thought to herself.

"Move aside," he asked Becca. Kyle stretched out his hand and put it through the mirror. Then he extended his leg and pushed it through the mirror as well.

Kyle was now standing in the middle of the mirror with half of his body visible to Jordan and Becca and the other half inside the mirror, on the other side of the portal. Jordan and Becca stood watching him. They were astonished. They stared at him as if they had seen a ghost and it was justified because this was not a normal, everyday occurrence for any of them.

The sight before them was something beyond the perception of the human mind.

Kyle walked out again. *"See? I'm not lying. Come, follow me."*

At first, both of them stared at Kyle as he passed through until he was no longer visible, then Jordan followed Kyle. After watching the two vanish through the mirror, Becca went in as well.

As they walked into this peculiar world, Jordan and Becca marveled at what they saw with their eyes wide open. They looked at themselves with disbelief and pinched their arms to see if they were real, too.

This time, Kyle felt more courageous than before. He knew he had the support of his two best friends even though they were now experiencing the same wave of overwhelming emotions that he felt when he had first looked at the forest around him. Jordan stumbled upon a stone and fell with a loud thud.

"Hush, be careful. There are creatures in this forest," said Kyle.

Without making any noise and walking close to each other, they kept walking on a clear path. The road was long, but their curiosity forced them to not give up. At this point, all the fear had left them as they anticipated the end of the pathway. They could not figure out if it were evening or afternoon, so Becca glanced at her watch. She was shocked to see that the hands of the watch did not move. The watch had stopped. She turned to Jordan to ask about the time; he told her his watch was not working either.

They were somewhat worried because they had to return home, but they did not want to turn back when a cave of undiscovered treasure that lay ahead of them. Finally, the end of the pathway arrived. There was an entire city laid out before their eyes. People were going about their day, talking to each other. Children played as if they had no idea that there was another world beyond the mirror. They seemed just as clueless as the people in the real world, and everything seemed too normal here.

It was a marvelous sight of city life for the three friends. They captured every detail as if they feared that this vision would soon disappear if they blinked. They walked in among the people to blend in and not be spotted, but no one looked at them suspiciously. They were too occupied to care where Jordan, Kyle, and Becca had come from.

Becca tried to stop people and ask what place it was, but no one stopped to answer. They were dressed up in normal clothes around the same era, which meant that there was no possibility of time traveling. It also did not look like a city of aliens or strange looking people. Everything was very ordinary, and that made it difficult for them to understand the differences on their own. They had to find out where they were and who the people were, but to do this; they had to inquire from the people in such a way that they would not suspect them to be outsiders.

Kyle, Jordan, and Becca had spent enough time being renegades in the society, and now, upon finding this new city, they were intrigued to know why this place even existed and how it came to be in the first place. Narcissism was at its peak in the real world. Everyone was so greedy that these three had withdrawn from the societies' standards and sought to establish their own little world of imagination. However, this was not an imaginary world. It was a real world, just as real as the one they had come out of, or at least it seemed to be. They needed to find out how this place was different from the place they had come from. In their search, Becca continued to think about what time it was, hoping they were not getting late to return home.

"Excuse me, can you tell me what time it is?" she asked an old woman passing by.

The woman was dressed up in a white and red plaid dress and had a smile on her face. The wrinkles on her face showed signs of very old age. Hearing Becca's question, she giggled as if she had said something bizarre. Becca became confused because all she had asked for was the time.

Jordan and Kyle thought that, perhaps, they spoke another language in the city, and that is why the woman could not understand what Becca had said. Another possible situation could be that the woman had a hearing impairment and so she could not figure out what Becca was trying to ask. Thus, they didn't pay much attention to it and moved on.

Next, they followed down the road that sloped towards these little houses which looked like scattered cardboard boxes from afar. This place sure didn't seem too advanced. There were people dressed up in normal attire, not too fancy or flamboyant. The houses were the size of just about what was needed. There were no enormous skyscrapers, occupying space for no reason. There were wide smiles on everyone's faces, and a unique peace reflected from their eyes. They seemed to be unstirred or unbothered by any worry of the world. There were beautiful plants and trees of every kind planted beside the houses.

Herbs and flowers hung by the windows of the small buildings, and streetlights came on one by one as the sun set over the city. They could make out that it was evening, but they decided not to go back home at this hour. They had come too far to look behind. Even if they did return the next day, they would have to go through the same long road again to finally make it to this populated area. Furthermore, returning at this hour of the day could prove to be quite dangerous for them, as Kyle knew that there were wild animals in the forest at the mirror's location.

In this new city, the roads were clear, and children were riding their bicycles without fears. As the sunlight blended in with the blue color of the sky, the light reflected on the glossy facades of the buildings. The city looked utterly magnificent. The three kept wandering in the streets, observing the people until it was almost nighttime.

At this hour, they came to a plain area where they saw a bunch of people camping beside a bonfire. They were talking in different languages, not just one, but they did know how to speak English. Kyle, Jordan, and Becca stood watching them from afar when one of the people who were camping beckoned them to join. Jordan and Becca were a little reluctant in trusting these people, especially at this time of night. They were in a place where they did not know the people, the customs, the culture, and not even their language.

They could not be friends with just anyone as these people could be murderers for all they knew. Whatever it was, they had no other choice, because they also needed a place to rest at night. It was true that the real world from where they came had instilled paranoia in their hearts. In the real world, everyone kept themselves aloof from the people they did not know and avoided any unnecessary interaction.

There was a lack of friendship, and the kind of acceptance with which the new people treated them was rare. Jordan held Kyle by the shirt as if to warn him of the consequences. Nevertheless, the three joined the little group of people and quietly sat on the stones on the ground. No one inquired where they had come from. Nobody knew them, but they all treated Kyle and his friends like revered guests.

The food and drinks offered to them were just as ordinary as what they ate in the real world. There was absolutely nothing here that seemed magical or unreal to the senses. The people then retreated to their respective camps giving these three an empty camp to spend the night. They spread a cloth on the ground and lay down, gazing at the stars above.

Where were they? What was this strange city? Everything seemed ordinary, but something was surely strange about this place. They needed to find out about this undiscovered land, this unknown city. The tranquility of the skies soothed their minds. They looked at the twinkling stars with dream-filled eyes. This could be a dream, but they wanted to enjoy it for as long as it lasted.

Chapter 9 – City Of Calamity

All the months that Kyle had spent with his two best friends, Jordan and Becca, were like a rollercoaster ride that stored many thrilling, wild experiences. They had made so many memories playing, exploring, and just having the time of their lives. Even in seclusion from the rest of the world, each other's company was more than enough for them. They knew that together, they could conquer every obstacle in life. They believed that the universe had conspired to bring them together so they could achieve anything that they wanted in life.

It was true that life had treated all three friends harshly, albeit in different ways, but now that they were together, everything seemed fun. They were happy despite the difficulties. They learned how to draw strength and comfort from each other and to encourage each other when lost all reason to keep going. There was one major problem that their generation faced: the young children were misunderstood, and their parents thought little about how their actions could impact the lives of their kids. The parents busied themselves in daily tasks and failed to understand the issues that bothered the young minds of their children. It was the same with these three friends, but now that they had each other, they felt understood. They had faced every situation head-on, but they had no idea what challenges awaited them. They looked at life with a different perspective and believed that no harm would come their way – at least none that they were not capable of handling on their own.

In Fountain Alley, everything was like it had always been. People continued living in narcissism and hatred towards one another. Materialism was everywhere, trapping people much like the quicksand that had caught Kyle the day he found the mirror. He had accidentally stepped inside the mire, but it had engulfed and imprisoned him. That quicksand was an apt representation of how materialism had ensnared people; it was drawing them towards destruction.

People were caught in the chains of materialism, and they could not free themselves – they didn't even realize they were chained! The saddest part was that Kyle, Jordan, and Becca had been the ones standing at the foot of the puddle of narcissism, extending their hands to pull others out, but people had refused to trust them. They were entirely unwilling to discard their greed and choose a better way out – a way that benefited not only them but all of humanity. It seemed as though it were too late to do anything – well, not unless everybody consented to bring the much-needed transformation. These three heroes still wished to bring change; despite the odds they faced, the three believed that, sooner or later, they would witness a revolution in the corrupt system of humanity. Until that happened, Fountain Valley would remain the same, unchanged, city of vain dreamers, a place where people were preoccupied with the surface than with what lay hidden underneath the appearances.

At home, Mrs. Williams seemed the least bothered about Kyle. Her son had told her of his plans to camp with his friends. He had not mentioned when, but she assumed that it was the reason why Kyle had not returned home that night. Even Jordan's parents did not contact him, and Becca was already staying alone at home, so there was no one to inquire about her whereabouts. The three friends knew full well that they were not going to get into any trouble with their parents even if they failed to make it home in the next two days. Their main concern was to find out where they were now.

The questions of what place it was, how so many people had managed to populate it, and how the portal was first created continued to perplex the three friends. It kept them up for the rest of the night. The people in the camps slept soundly while these three remained wide awake like night owls. They began discussing theories regarding the existence of this hidden world. They shared their ideas about the place and its people. They found comfort in the fact that at least they were in it together. Wherever they were being led, it surely had a purpose for them. However, they had no clue what their next step would be. Whispering to each other under the starry sky, they witnessed the sunrise. After hours of discussions and planning, they finally fell asleep.

The morning was stranger than what they had expected it to be. Becca woke up to the sound of people's voices. She kept her eyes closed, and listened intently to what those voices were saying, trying to figure out the meaning behind their words. The language seemed foreign once again. She shot up straight and began to look around the place. In her sleep, she had forgotten where they were. She felt as if she had been sleeping in her room, only the grass on which she lay chafed against her skin and was a bit uncomfortable. She glanced at Jordan and Kyle, who was still sound asleep, unconscious of the world and its worries. The people in the camps were packing their bags as if they were setting out on a journey to some other place. Becca lay down again as she saw the people walking away. It seemed like they were nomads moving from one place to another, either for exploration, or to look for something. What was weird was that these people did not bother to wake them up. As they set out walking towards a hill located far away, Becca tapped Kyle's shoulder. *"Wake up, Kyle! Wake up!"*

He shifted to his side and did not wake up.

"Jordan! Wake up!" Becca said, shaking his shoulder now to wake him from his deep sleep.

Jordan squinted as the daylight pierced into his eyes. By looking at the sun, one could tell that it was afternoon, which meant that they had been sleeping for a very long time. Kyle also awoke slowly, rubbing his eyes to push sleep away. They looked around in confusion, clearly expecting to find people around them.

Becca explained, *"The people just packed their bags and left. They went to the hilly areas."*

"They did look like hikers to me," said Kyle.

"Yeah, and the way they spoke in different languages may be because they were from different parts of the city," said Jordan.

"I wonder how many languages are spoken here," said Kyle.

The questions piled up in their heads – and they had no way of finding answers. One question after another popped up in their minds, but all of them went unanswered as they remained clueless about what this place was. They could not rely on their own understanding, but they were noting down all the strange things that were happening around them – things such as the absence of clocks and watches to track the time. Even the watches they had, such as Becca's watch, had stopped working as soon as they had stepped into this world.

Another strange thing was the way people acted. They were busy in their everyday lives, unaware of what the real world was going through. They seemed happy and content, which was contrary to the common human nature that these three were accustomed to seeing in the real world.

Becca, Jordan, and Kyle got up and stretched. In no time at all, they were all set to embark on the journey to explore this tiny planet. They had to find out more about this place. The three started walking down towards the road, the area where houses were located. They needed to find someone who spoke the same language so they could learn something about this place. As they walked in the streets, they found that the ground was very clean, especially the lanes which separated all the short, squat buildings from one another.

The three friends could tell that there were far fewer people in this city than in Fountain Alley or any other place in their homeland. The population was relatively small; however, even amongst the people who were milling about, they could not spot anybody who displayed narcissistic characteristics. They were all too nice and understanding towards each other and life. Here, you could find meaning in things and purity in people's intentions.

All of this truly was too good to be true, and perhaps this was the reason why their minds were constantly questioning what they had been experiencing. They continued walking in the streets and observed the people who were occupied in their daily chores. The women stood in the balcony pinning the washed clothes to the clotheslines. Groups of carefree children were playing with each other. They also saw people petting their animals, and treat them with kindness, as though they were God's precious creation – which they were. Where was the materialism now? Where did the narcissism go? This, of course, made the three friends glad. This was unlike anything they had seen before. They had only heard of times when narcissism's grip on human nature was still not as deathly – and now, they saw it with their own eyes.

Nevertheless, it also seemed strange to them to see so many 'empaths,' as their psychology teacher called them, in one place and at the same time. Not one person they saw displayed the horrible attitude of selfishness and self-centeredness. The sight before them made them very glad; it looked as if their plan had been executed. Even as they were happy, they were worried about their own families and people that they had left behind on the other side of the mirror. They wanted to go back and tell them to be like the people of this city, but nobody would believe them.

Becca, Jordan, and Kyle decided to part ways so they could go around and explore more of the city than they could roam around as one group. Kyle had the job of looking for a place where they could stay so they did not have to spend another night under the sky with the constant fear of being attacked, although this idea seemed to be impossible in this city. Jordan had the task of finding out some details about the place, and Becca had to do the same as well. The three went their different ways so they could discover and learn as much as possible about this place.

Kyle went to a nearby hotel that seemed to be located in the middle of shops and restaurants. The restaurants were not too lavish; they were just small places, big enough to accommodate a few groups of people for lunch, dinner, or sharing a few cups of coffee.

When Kyle saw the hotel located in the cramped up space, he decided to go inside and ask if he and his friends could get a room. Walking up the stairs, he found a man who asked for details about his stay and, after some queries, allowed him to have a room at the top floor to where they could stay for as long as they wanted. They were very young so the hotel manager, a short man, went easy on them and did not even ask for payment. No one looked on the three kids with suspicion in their eyes, and this was great because it meant they could blend easily with the crowd. Kyle stayed in the area; he stood on the road and waited because they had planned to meet at the same spot after they were done exploring.

Meanwhile, Jordan, who was supposed to go and talk to people to inquire, spent most of his time marveling at the various sights he came across. He sat with the children who were playing and joined them. He even sat in a vacant coffee shop and observed the people passing by on the road outside. Well, that too, was a great way to investigate this place. People seemed too engrossed in their work. Jordan just watched them come and go quietly without intervening in any manner.

The weather was warm, and sweat beads formed on Jordan's forehead, which he wiped away with the back of his hand. There were no air conditioners in the place, and a few fans dangled from the ceiling to cool off the heat. There were no lavish appliances here at all, Jordan observed, but only a few necessary ones. Even the people seemed to be unstirred by the absence of technology. They were content with the life they were living and seemed to find much joy in the little things in life. The smiles on their faces were also not fake or plastered on just for the sake of exhibition. Their smiles seemed genuine and hopeful, unaffected by the worries of the world. Jordan, worn out by walking for hours on the streets, finally decided to go back to the main meeting spot where Kyle awaited him.

As soon as they met, Kyle informed him about the room, and Jordan also narrated what happened on his hunt for clues. Becca had not returned yet. She might have found something that could lead them towards the root of the issue, they determined. Becca was an intelligent girl, but more than that, she was always firm about getting things done. They had faith that Becca would return with helpful clues and answers.

After surveying through the other side of the streets, Becca had decided to go to a place where more camps had been set up. The group of people that had put up the camp stood at a distance; Becca could tell they were engrossed in some discussion. A girl who also seemed to be a part of that group sat on a large stone, all by herself. Becca thought it was a great opportunity to talk to her and find out something about this place. The girl had her face down on her lap as she stared carefully at the ground, searching for something. Becca walked up to her. The girl looked up, startled by the sound of Becca's shoes. She looked at Becca who felt as if she had woken up the girl from a deep sleep. The girl had tears in her eyes, so she looked away and hid her face. Becca could see that something was troubling her. The girl was a little older than Becca, but her short bob haircut made her look younger than she was.

As soon as she saw Becca, she began fidgeting with her hair out of anxiety. She started tapping her foot and smiled awkwardly to hide whatever pain she was going through. Becca sat next to the girl, and without allowing the silence to continue, she said, *"Hi, my name is Becca."* She gave a smile of reassurance to build a rapport with the girl.

The girl stretched out her arm to shake hands and said in a low voice, *"Miley."* She did not say anything other than her name, which clearly showed that she did not want to continue talking.

Becca still sat there next to her. *"What happened? Are you okay?"* she asked.

"I don't know..." said Miley, looking away to the other side to hide her face.

"It's all right," said Becca, patting on her back to comfort her. Miley buried her face in her hands and began sobbing. Becca, unsure of what to say next, asked her to speak her heart and talk about whatever was troubling her.

Miley continued sobbing and sniffling and then said, *"Let's move away from this place. If they see me talking to a stranger, they will get really mad."*

Becca was confused about who Miley was referring to; nevertheless, she stood up, dusted off her jeans, and waited for Miley to respond. They had no idea where they were going. Becca insisted that she come with her to where Jordan and Kyle were waiting.

"My friends are waiting, too. Why don't you come and meet them? Also, you can talk to me on the way," said Becca, smiling at Miley, who smiled back.

They kept walking, turning to see the people who were at the camp to check if someone had seen them talking, but no one had seen them. So they walked down towards the lane that led to the hotel.

"I can't get over the loss, Becca. I just can't," said Miley. Becca wondered what the loss was.

"They say I should forget, but I can't. After the destruction, I am not able to forget my mother and sister; I still hear their voices in my head. I want to go back, but they are not letting me go."

Becca was astonished as she sensed that something was wrong with the world they had known as home for all this time.

"Um, it's okay, Miley. I understand," said Becca, pretending to know what Miley was talking about.

Miley began to sob again. She wiped off her tears by the sleeve of her shirt. Becca did not know how to tell her that she had no clue what she was talking about. She had no idea how to let Miley know she and her friends had entered through the portal into this strange world.

Becca quietly listened to her, hoping to find out more details on their way to the hotel. She did not want to freak Miley out, at least not so soon. They walked down the street where Kyle and Jordan stood, both of whom heaved a sigh of relief as they watched Becca walking towards them.

Chapter 10 – Two Sides

Becca walked slowly towards Jordan and Kyle, who stood at the corner of the street. They looked perplexed but also glad to see that Becca had convinced someone in this city to be her friend. Perhaps this girl could help them figure something out about this place. At the same time, they were a little cautious because they could not just trust anyone blindly. They knew nothing about this world so they could not trust the judgments of their minds.

Even though everyone here seemed happy and harmless, they could secretly be observing them and plotting against them. What if the people on this side were conspiring against the people of the other side? There were so many questions rushing through their minds that only Miley could answer, but how would they be able to ask questions in such a way that she would not suspect that these three did not even belong to the same place? Kyle and Jordan began to think of excuses and stories as the girls walked up to them.

"Hey, Becca," said Kyle, *"Where were you?"*

"I was just walking down the street when I met Miley,"

Becca replied. She did not reveal how she saw her crying because she did not want Miley to feel awkward amongst a bunch of strangers. She was trying her best to make her feel comfortable in their company. *"Miley, this is Kyle, and this is Jordan,"* Becca pointed towards them as they awkwardly smiled.

Miley smiled too, but her smiled changed into a straight face almost quickly, letting them know she had only smiled as a formality. *"Hey,"* she managed to utter through her thin, dry lips.

Her face should clear signs of crying, or maybe she was dehydrated. She was pale and tired, which made her look gaunt, and also younger.

"Hey, please come upstairs," Kyle pointed towards the hotel stairs, which led to the room he had booked for their night stay.

The people outside the hotel still did not pay any attention to who they were. They were busy passing by in the streets or caught up in their work. They seemed to be unconcerned and untroubled by anything that went around them. Leading up the stairs, Becca seemed pretty impressed by how quickly these guys had arranged a place. Earlier, she had doubted they could get a place to rest for the night and had dreaded the idea of sleeping out in the open once again. Kyle still had not forgotten that he had heard loud growls of a wild animal at the entrance of the woods. It could be dangerous to spend another night camping outside. They were glad they had found a place; the room was too small as one could already expect by looking at how small the hotel was. The hotel manager glanced at them and busied himself in writing something on the paper.

All four of them went into the room and sat on the comfy bed. The room was warm, and the small window allowed some air for ventilation, but overall, it was not as bad as it was outside. After all, it was just a matter of another night, or God forbid, a few more days, which they did not even want to imagine. Even though no one cared at home, it would not have been a wise choice to stay here. One other reason was that they had no money to pay for the room – and how long could they stay here rent free? They wanted to leave as soon as possible, but at the same time, they wanted to find out what was going on in this city.

"Why are you guys staying here?" asked Miley. *"Didn't they give you a place to stay?"*

"Um, no…" hesitated Jordan, as he looked towards Becca to answer. He was afraid to say anything, fearing it might reveal that they did not belong here. Becca hesitated too because she had not thought of a story that she could tell Miley.

She just said, *"No, we've just been "*

"Oh, have you guys recently moved from the camps, too?" said Miley before Becca could finish her sentence. *"Today, was my last day at the camp, I'll get a place in few days."* They were all confused about what she was talking about – what were these camps and who were these people? Was it the government? Everything was too vague, and they dared not ask any questions at present.

A long moment of silence prevailed as they all looked at each other, thinking of the situation they were in. Miley seemed a little comfortable as she began talking. They were quite friendly and seemed completely harmless. What could these young children do, after all?

"Uh... Miley," said Becca in a low voice. Becca had mustered the courage to tell her everything about herself and her friends. They could no longer delay the conversation and pretend to be a part of Miley's world. They had to be honest, regardless of what it took. Becca was willing to take the risk, and she had high hopes that it would not result in disappointment.

"Miley, I don't know what you're talking about, okay? I have no clue what is going on," she grimaced, prepared for an outburst of anger and defense.

"What? What do you mean?" asked Miley, clearly unable to understand what was going on.

"Miley, please do not freak out. We are not spies or intruders. We are just kids who happened to come across this place," said Becca. Miley listened closely, the stress lines on her forehead more relaxed now. Becca's calm voice instilled a feeling of reassurance in her.

"Wait, Let me explain," said Becca, getting up from the squeaking old wood chair to check if the door was closed; she didn't want anybody to accidentally overhear or eavesdrop on their conversation. They were alert at all times

because they could not afford being caught as criminals when they were innocent. They could not risk Miley's life either though she was a part of this world.

"We are from the other side. We do not belong here," said Becca.

Jordan and Kyle stole a glance at each other, each waiting to see Miley's reaction.

"I do not belong here either," said Miley as she lowered her gaze. It looked as if she were suddenly touched by sadness.

"No, I mean… yeah sure, you must be from the other side, but the thing is we entered on our own. No one knows us, but we want to know what is going on here because everything we have come across so far is so confusing," said Becca.

"How did you'll enter?" Miley asked in astonishment.

"The glass mirror in the woods," added Kyle. *"I found it while we were playing in the forest next to my house. It's a portal through which we entered this place, and now we are lost. What even is this place?"*

"Are you serious? Is there a portal? That means that it can also be an escape!" Miley said, jumping in her place. Her eyes burned with the fires of hope as she heard them talk about the existence of a portal. They added more details and narrated the entire account of how they had spent their day here and told Miley about the people they had met. They bombarded her with questions about herself and wanted to know why the people here act so weirdly.

"Well, listen carefully," Miley whispered, looking around the room in fear though they were alone. She lowered her voice, as though she was afraid even of the walls hearing her. *"Guys, you have made a mistake coming here. You will be surprised to find out what is going on."*

"What?" Jordan said.

"This place is not an ordinary place. It has been specially prepared by scientists. We are all a part of an experiment," Miley revealed.

"What sort of experiment?" asked Becca.

"The world outside from where you guys have come is under the threat of being destroyed by the epidemic of narcissism. Scientists and psychologists have secretly been

trying to find a way to control this. They created a chemical which can numb the people's minds and fix them on focusing and enjoying even the smallest, most trivial things in life."

"Woah, now that's interesting," said Kyle, overjoyed at the news that there was something like the technology Miley had just talked about. The subject of narcissism had long been on his mind. To learn that experiments and studies were underway on this subject was very fascinating to him!

"This is not a good thing, Kyle. These people, every one of us, are being fed with this chemical. But the worst part is that they have forcefully taken us. No one knows where we are, not even our families. The people close to being destroyed have been left alone, while we, on this side of the world, are being treated like lab rats to see if this chemical could work," said Miley.

"So, is it working?" asked Kyle.

"Well, yes, on most of the people. But it did not work on me. The people whose minds do not need to be cured are still the same. This experiment is destructive because these people want to destroy that world and create a new earth here. This is not real; all of this is forced. We will just be

living robotic lives with no emotions of our own. They are not eradicating narcissism, but controlling people," said Becca.

"The world on the other side needs help, but forcing people to be busy by thinking only about trivial things and forgetting their families and the issues that they are leaving behind is downright evil. Also, they plan on creating this place so that they could move here once the entire planet is destroyed, and it no longer holds life. They will just start afresh in this city."

"This is messed up," said Jordan, shaking his head in disbelief.

"This is an evil plan that must be stopped at all costs."

"Yes, but who would do that? The only key is to escape from the same place where you guys came from," said Miley.

"They are bringing more and more people in this place. Soon enough they will find out about you guys, too. So the safest way is to run away before they find you. You guys must inform the people outside or stop this process somehow."

The three friends were astounded to learn of the situation. This place was not as safe as they had thought it was, and now, they felt bad about the victims of the experiment. *"That is why the people were acting so strange all this time, "* said Kyle.

"Oh yeah, and what about the time? Why are there no clocks or watches here?" asked Becca. They were all thinking about everything now that may have happened to this place. They were analyzing things very carefully to make sense of it all.

"That is because they do not want people to keep any track of time. They want the people to just focus on the little things in life and not be controlled even by the necessity of time, " said Miley.

"Oh, God, all of this is just making me feel sick, " said Becca.

"It is unbelievable; why are people doing this? Are you alone here, Miley? Do you know anyone else?"

"No. My family, my mother, and my sister are on the other side. They just took me while the others are going to be destroyed..." Miley sobbed as she spoke.

"We are not going to leave you alone here, Miley, " said Kyle. *"We are going help every one of these people to*

escape. "

"It is not safe, guys. You all should leave this place today. Maybe come back tomorrow, but do not stay here for the night because if they find out that you have not been through the experiment but are just living with us, then they are going to cage you and make you a part of this. I do not want you guys to suffer," said Miley.

"I'll have to leave, too. I'll probably meet you guys here again whenever you come back. I have been gone for too long, and they must be looking for me. I'm glad I met you guys, and I hope to see you all soon. Stay safe!" Miley hurried towards the door and unlatched it. They followed her and accompanied her down the stairs.

The manager gave them a weird look again as if he could sense that something was seriously wrong with them. They brushed off the look and told themselves that the manager had no way of knowing who they were and where they had come from.

As Miley, the three of them walked upstairs again and shut themselves in the room. They were amazed at what Miley had told them, her words resounded in their memory because it was not something normal. How could someone devise such an evil plan? How could such a thing even happen in the first place? Everything that Miley had told them was mindboggling, and they took their time to let the truth sink in. The world outside was evil, and so were the people who were carrying out these experiments.

They must have thought that it was a great strategy, but in reality, it was all demonic. This was not the way to solve the problem of narcissism. This was not the cure; they could not leave the people to destruction and create a new planet. The three friends were troubled, and they knew that they were going to spend another sleepless night in the comfort of the four walls. Their newly discovered knowledge would not permit them to sleep in peace.

Lying there, Kyle thought back to the time when it had all started. Who knew that someone could think of an evil strategy like the one practiced in this strange city? Kyle was not only worried about the planet to which they belonged but his family too. He could not leave behind his mother, father, and sister to be destroyed by narcissism. As Kyle closed his eyes, he saw his mother's image smiling at him. He could almost hear her voice…the way she had sounded on the night she had shared precious lessons about life with him. He could also not forget everyone back at the school, either. Even though they were under narcissism's effect, Kyle was still very empathetic toward them. He remembered his dreams too, the one in which he was flying while the people looked up at him. He could not just leave multitudes to be devoured by narcissism. He wanted to rescue all of them and tell them where the problem truly lay.

A deep conviction rang deep in his heart. He closed his eyes and fell asleep. They had not slept properly the day before so he could not keep himself awake though he wanted to think of their current predicament some more. Becca and Jordan, on the other hand, talked about their day. Trying to distract each other from reality, they began talking about funny incidences from school.

Thinking about home also made them a little emotional, and they could understand what Miley was going through. They had not been too involved with their families because of their behavior, but they deeply understood the consequences of abandoning the people they loved the most. They could not even bear the thought of doing that. All three of the friends wanted to make the world a better place, but they knew this wasn't the way to go about it. They had to take a step to put a halt to this bizarre plan that had imprisoned so many unsuspecting people in this strange city. They thought of leaving first, to go back and warn the people out there and inform them about this place.

They had to return to the portal and pass right through before it was too late and before all the alternate routes to freedom were destroyed. It felt like they were caught up in some sort of labyrinth of confusion and chaos – and they knew they had to find a way back home as soon as they could.

Chapter 11 – Closed Road

Miley's explanation of what was going in this strange world had left the three friends scared and confused. They feared for their lives and were afraid that something terrible might happen if they stayed there for another day. It wasn't that they were terrified only of the deadly consequences, but they wanted to escape the city as they were the last hope for the innocent people who were suffering. They could not risk staying back in any case. In addition to the suffering of the people here, they were extremely worried about their families that they had left behind on the other side.

They had no clue what was going on at the other end. *What would my mother be doing right now?* Kyle wondered. He thought about the mundane, repetitive life he lived back at home. He imagined his mom cooking in the kitchen, and then leaving for work. Was everything happening the way it always did or had the chaotic epidemic of narcissism worsened things? He could not bear the thought of a world without his mother. Then, as he thought of his dad, his heart filled with more love. He knew that, after all the ill-treatment that people showed, deep inside, some parts of their souls were full of goodness. They deserved love and affection just as much, and it was only a matter of some hard work to make them realize where they were wrong.

"We cannot stay here for another night, guys," insisted Kyle.

"We must leave right at dawn and return to where the portal is located before they find out about us. Pick up all your belongings and make sure we leave nothing which would help them in finding us."

"I wonder if Miley has reached back safely," said Becca. She empathized with Miley, but she felt helpless. There was nothing she could do to help her new friend.

"We have to return as soon as possible so that we can save these people. Every passing minute is just adding to my anxiety," said Jordan.

Every passing minute was precious. The night was calm; silence echoed in the streets, their hearts raced as they attempted their great escape. By the look of the sky outside, it must have been around five in the morning. The three packed their bags, and double checked the room to see if they had left anything behind. Then, they walked down the creaky staircase and looked around to see if there was someone who would catch them going outside. The path was clear; even the man at the reception slept soundly. His snores were so loud that they could be heard outside as they walked out the main door. The way out was narrow, so they had to be careful to avoid making any noise that would wake the receptionist up. First, Jordan stepped out, then Becca, and in the end, Kyle, who closed the door behind him as quietly as possible.

Outside, strong winds blew that sent shivers down their spine. It was dark at the moment, but they knew that by the time they would reach the woods, the sun would rise. It was the perfect plan; they could not go during the day because the residents could easily spot them and probably be caught if they realized the three did not belong there.

For now, the sun seemed like an enemy that could bring the truth to light, so they accepted darkness as a cloak in which they could hide as they hurried down the lanes. After walking for miles, they finally reached the forest they had come into this world from. The tall trees looked scarier than one could imagine in the dark. Who knew what danger must be waiting for them in this dense forest that already had so many secrets hidden within its shadows? It was not a safe place either, but neither was the city. The people were more dangerous than wild animals. The animals attacked people because they had to eat something to survive, or for self-defense. But then, what was the cause of man's inhuman behavior? What caused them to be heartless creatures that only knew how to mindlessly pursue their selfish interest?

The so-called scientists of this city were doing nothing for the welfare of the people as they implied. In fact, they were destroying the creation of God and establishing an entirely new world, ruining the lives of all the people who they planned to leave behind on the other side. Walking down the path, through the woods that lead to the mirror, the three friends stuck close together and looked around cautiously at every turn to avoid any danger.

Finally, they reached the place where the mirror was located. Magnificently placed amid the oak trees, the mirror glowed with a strange light. How could one possibly overlook it and walk away? They heaved a sigh of relief because now they could finally escape. They glanced at one another, and Kyle stepped forward first to pass through the portal. Kyle walked towards the mirror but hit his head against the glass. Worried, Kyle ran back and forward, smashing himself into the mirror.

"What the heck? The mirror isn't working?" said Jordan.

Kyle tried again and again, but the portal was now closed. There was no way out of this place other than this mirror – at least none that they knew of – and now, unfortunately, the mirror was not working anymore. While they anxiously tried to escape, they suddenly heard whispers from behind the trees. It was dawn, the sun had risen, and the light peered through the dense leaves, throwing a reflection on the mirror. The voices slowly became more audible, and the three pulled themselves back from the woods.

It was still quite dark for them to find out who was there, but by the voices they heard, they could figure out that they were many people. Suddenly, they heard loud growls. Kyle realized this was the same growling noise that he had heard when he had first entered into this dark world. Out from the cover of the trees stepped two massive creatures that looked like dragons. Their eyes were like alligators' shifty eyes; the texture and color of their skin helped them camouflage themselves well in the dark.

This was why their features seemed unclear to the three friends. The dragon-like creatures seemed dangerous and not friendly at all. They were horrifying, and the way they stared at the three made it look like they were going to swallow them whole. Sweat dripped down their foreheads as they breathed heavily at the terrible sight of the large beasts. They only had two choices; either they could pretend to be dead, which would have been the most foolish method of survival to apply here, or they could run for their lives. But how could they run? Their legs were shaking with fear, and their bodies went cold. They were paralyzed and failed to make a move.

However, they also knew full well that there was someone else besides these creatures, hiding amid all these trees. It was not an animal, and they were certain about that. It was a human presence behind the trees, and they had to escape from, both, man and beast.

As another growl reached their ears, Kyle shouted, *"Run!"*

The three of them ran towards the left, trusting their intuition to find a safe place. They kept running through the dark. They did not know where they were going; their only motive was to escape death. It is weird how living beings try to give their all when their lives are in danger, and even when escape seems impossible. Yet, they try their hardest to survive, to defeat death, or to avoid it as long as they can. The branches of the trees hindered them from running as fast as they wanted. They even slashed their arms against the undergrowth and fell into the muddy ground several times, only to get back up on their feet and resume running. They continued sprinting to the east to escape their doom, which seemed more inevitable by the minute.

Intense lights of torches chased them. Along with the intermittent growls, the sound of a helicopter made them more and more confused. Whoever the people were, they were surveying the woods to spot the three friends. It seemed like someone had informed them about their presence, or maybe someone had found the mirror.

They did not have time to think about what was happening. All they could do was to keep running and save their lives. As they ran, Kyle fell, and his foot got stuck in the brushwood. He could not pull his foot loose from the thorny bed of plants because it was extremely painful. At first, Becca and Jordan could not figure out what had happened with Kyle, but then they looked behind and saw

Kyle writhing in pain. The voices had calmed down by now, and it seemed like they had left their hunters behind. They stopped and helped Kyle stand up from the dirt and comforted him. As they stood up, around four to five people, clothed in black, came and seized them. They immediately handcuffed the three of them as they screamed at the top of their lungs.

"Help! Help!" they cried.

There was going to be no help for them. The people who had caught them kept talking to each other in a foreign language; the trio couldn't understand what they were saying, but the tone of the voice told them that instructions were being imparted. Then three more people in masks came forward from behind the woods and injected them. A rushing sensation ran through their blood, and their bodies fell weak.

All they could see were blurred images and the bright sunlight that made its way through the canopy of the trees. The people's voices also grew dim. Soon, the three friends' bodies began to go numb and limp. They were slowly losing control over their thoughts as well, which was more frightening to them than anything else. The people who had seized them lay them down on stretchers and loaded them in a car. The last sight that Kyle witnessed was a face masked in black, pushing him down on the stretcher; black covered his vision, and he lost all consciousness. Hour – or maybe days – passed. Kyle regained consciousness slowly. He found himself in a completely foreign place. He was still dizzy, and he knew that must be because of the injection that had put all three of them to sleep.

He looked around, and he could see his friends lying next to him. They were on a bed that looked like a hospital bed, and their hands and feet were chained to the iron railings. They were in a lab; perhaps the same lab where experiments were conducted on the human population. The lab was brightly lit – the artificial lights were so bright Kyle felt blinded by them.

As his two friends lay unconscious on their beds, Kyle sent a sweeping glance through the place. There was a gleaming stainless steel table on which rested various tools. There were chemical bottles which contained toxic liquids that gave off pungent fumes. Also, large cupboards and cabinets lined the walls that seemed to be made of steel. One could tell that there was a great project that these people were working on; it definitely did not look like it was yesterday's work. As Kyle turned his face upwards, still lying down, he saw glass walls through which another room could be seen. These walls were covered with equations which were written down in black and blue markers. This was certainly a well-crafted plan. Suddenly, Kyle heard footsteps in the hallway; he closed his eyes and pretended to be asleep. The footsteps became clearer as a man stepped inside; Kyle saw he was wearing a white lab coat from the corner of his eye.

His hair was straight and neatly gelled to one side. He was tall and slender with gold-framed glasses on his pale face. From his appearance, the man looked very sophisticated, and the way he walked showed discipline and sternness. He looked like a scientist who was too focused on his duties and was here to carry out a great experiment. Two men and a woman, neatly clothed in white, followed the first man.

One of the men was short and skinny with the same pale looking skin that, by now, seemed like the side effects of staying in the lab. Kyle continued to pretend to be asleep, peeking every now and then from the corner of his eyes. The first man filled another injection and stepped forward as if to give them another shot, but then he put the injection on a stainless steel tray that rested on the table next to Kyle.

"Prepare the rest of them and take these away," commanded the scientist. All this happened while they had been speaking in a foreign language, but for the first time, Kyle heard this person speak in English. The man spoke in a stern but low voice. He did not look cruel though his features were fixed like a sculpture. The men and the woman took hold of the three beds, which moved like trolleys and dragged them to another room.

Kyle kept quiet and observed what was happening around them. He was also scared because his friends were still unconscious. What if something had happened to them? He could not stand the thought of anything bad happening to them. How could he return home without them? He could not even imagine going back home alone and decided that he had to wake them up, but he could not rush things here. He knew he would have to be very cautious.

He had to be wise and patient about everything. The beds were taken to another strange-looking room which glowed with blue lights. Many other people were lying on the beds inside the room. Kyle became paralyzed with fear. The people lying on the bed were of different ages, but most of them were children of about the same age as Miley. All of them were sound asleep like Becca and Jordan. As Kyle observed the people and tried to recognize their faces, he felt helpless because he could not save them. He also felt utterly depressed as he looked at the pale faces glowing in the blue light. Their pale faces were not the ordinary kind of pale.

Their pallor made Kyle think that the blood had been drained from their bodies, and they had been frozen. The room was cold, but thankfully, it was not as cold as a morgue. The people were also alive, only they were in a temporary state of unconsciousness because of the strong effect of the chemicals. What a cruel act this was! How could someone inflict such pain on someone in the name of charity?

"Hey, psst...," someone whispered.

Again, Kyle closed his eyes and pretended to be asleep. He heard the same whisper in the next few seconds, and finally, he turned his head around. A boy was lying next to him, whom he had failed to notice.

"Who are you?" asked Kyle.

"I'm Troye. You?" he whispered.

"I'm Kyle, and these are my friends, Jordan and Becca."

"How did you end up here? I did not see you in the van when they abducted us, " said Troye.

"We came into this world through a mirror, and we found about these experiments from a girl named Miley. She warned us of the consequences and told us to return to the real world and help the people here to get out. Sadly, when we returned, the mirror had stopped working, and these people hunted us down in the woods as if we were criminals. "

"Oh no, " the boy said, looking horrified.

"Now we're here. We were the only hope for all these people because we could go back and stop this cruelty, but we failed, " Kyle finished.

Kyle began to cry as the feeling of helplessness overwhelmed him. The state of the people and his friends grieved him deeply, but he could do nothing at all to help them or to even help himself.

"Kyle, don't worry. It's going to be fine. We'll make it out of here, " said Troye.

"It's not the end; we're going to fight these people and stop this evil system, " Kyle looked at him with hope and

smiled.

"We can do it together. We can bring an end to this if we unite."

Troye was a 15-year-old who displayed the same vigor that they had against the evil in the world. Kyle was reminded of himself and his friends who wanted to bring a change in the society they lived in. They had surely failed in escaping on their own, but this time, Kyle decided to not give up. He was going to escape with everyone else who was trapped here.

The end was near, and Kyle knew they could not afford giving up at this point. They had not come so far to back down in fear. With patience, endurance, perseverance, and with strong unity among themselves, they could conquer the dark forces that had imprisoned them in this strange city. Troye had given him a renewed sense of much-needed hope amidst this hopeless situation, and Kyle once again felt invincible.

Chapter 12 – Don't Give Up

The cold air in the lab permeated through their skin and bit into their bones. Kyle and Troye lay helplessly among the rest of the subjects who were sound asleep due to the effects of the sedative. The chains at their feet held them all so tightly to their beds that struggling to release themselves would have surely left bruises on their skin. Even Kyle's ankle ached as the metal chain grazed against his skin every time he moved.

The cold helped to numb the pain. Troye was still a little dizzy, so he lay on his back against the stretcher. Kyle sat up, supporting his back using a pillow while surveying the room to find something with which to cut the chain at his feet, while Troye lay there motionless on his bed.

Kyle finally spotted a knife resting in a metal tray on a trolley next to a girl who was unconscious like the others. He dragged his trolley stealthily towards her; he was afraid to wake her up. Dragging the trolley was indeed a painful struggle because every time he pulled, the chain tugged at his feet. Kyle quickly grabbed the knife as he reached the trolley and began to cut the metal chain. Although there was no clock in the room, he had a mental estimation that time was running out. He placed the knife at one spot on the chain and began scraping it against the metal link like crazy.

The chain was not thick enough to make the process impossible. It was going to take a while, but eventually, Kyle knew he would dismantle it successfully. As he wrestled against the chain, he looked across the room every once in a while to make sure that no one was there to catch him. Troye, who was now lying a few steps away, observed him; he quietly hoped that Kyle would be free soon and liberate the rest of the captives, as well.

As Kyle continued his struggle, he had a sudden flashback from a dream that he had seen at home. He remembered floating in the air and drifting away from the people while they tugged at his feet. The feeling of being fastened to this chain was uncannily similar. He was shaken with astonishment as he contemplated if that dream was a prediction of the future. However, he also doubted if these feelings were strong because of the aftereffects of the sedative and that there was no special significance of that dream. Engrossed in his thoughts, Kyle did not realize that he had finally managed to break free from the chain. He quickly unfastened himself and ran towards Troye, who was now back in his senses. Also, the responsibility that they now shared of escaping the lab infused a sense of strength in him. Kyle opened Troye's chain as well, and they both went and unchained the fellow victims of the experiment. Every moment that passed increased the fear of being caught red-handed, but they had planned to attack their attackers with knives in case of emergency.

Troye ran and watched if there was someone in the corridor outside, but the entire place seemed to be empty. The rooms, adjacent to the room they were kept in, were locked. Troye wanted to make sure if the path was clear so that they would escape, but as soon as he heaved a sigh of relief, he glanced at a camera right above his head. Then he looked at the ceiling of the corridor and found that the place was filled with cameras, and they were being monitored. He immediately rushed back in because he feared someone had seen him walk down the hallway.

"Kyle, it won't be safe to go out right now. There are cameras everywhere," he said to Kyle.

"All right, let me think of *what else we can do,"* replied Kyle.

He was surprisingly calm at that moment. In his mind, he was mapping out a whole strategy for escape even though he did not know much about where the exit was. However, right now, he only cared about dodging the cameras and taking the captives away from this lab.

The cold was getting unbearable now, especially because they were up and conscious of their surroundings. They could not wait for long because if the people found out that they were awake, they would catch them again, thereby endangering their chances of escape.

Kyle and Troye concluded that they would go out and inform the people about this and later come to help these people. Kyle and Troye locked the door behind them and ran through the hallway so that no one would spot them. The hallway was followed by stairs that lead to two more doors. On one of them had a note posted on them that said: *"Do Not Enter."* Kyle became more curious than he already was on seeing the note. He slid the door open and entered the room. It was really big and had white walls. The entire place gave off a vibe of a hospital because of the instruments that were lying around. However, this room was relatively different. It was empty with just another metal door right at the end, which said, *"Exit."* It was strange how it suggested that no one may enter the room while there was nothing else but an exit door beyond that. However, it also made sense why they would not want anyone to come into this particular room. They entered through the exit door and what they saw left them utterly astonished.

The room was again empty and quite identical to the previous one, but there was a mirror lying at the end of the room. Kyle and Troye immediately looked at each other because they had found out the way to their homes again. Perhaps this was the mirror that was replaced by the scientists with the one that they had tried to escape from in the forest. As they walked towards it slowly, the mirror gleamed with the same strange blue light.

They had luckily found out the place which could lead them to their homeland, and they could now save the rest of the victims of this morbid experiment. This world has been a labyrinth for them, and a whole new mystery awaited them each step of the way. They had finally made it to the end because of their determination. Kyle had not given up, though he didn't have Jordan and Becca by his side. He missed them, and it was heart-wrenching to not being able to find them among the people in the room. This also meant that there was, perhaps, another room where more people were undergoing the process of experiment. But Kyle had to take that risk once again. Either he could let his emotions hold him back, or he could push those feelings aside and think rationally.

Kyle allowed Troye to walk out the mirror first, and then he followed. Another responsibility lay ahead at the other end: they had let people know about the experiment. The time had come for this rebellious group to expose the truth about the experiments being held in the other world that lay beyond the mirror.

Kyle did not have the support of his best friends right now, but he knew in his heart that they always had his back, and would love and support him even if the entire world turned against him. He had already faced so much opposition and criticism; however, Jordan and Becca had stuck with him through all the highs and lows. Though right now, he did not have his friends by his side, he did not want to weaken.

He resolved to not give up. All these thoughts were still running through his mind when they stepped across the portal. Both of them landed on a bed of grass. Kyle recognized that he was back in the forest next to his house and direct Troye towards his home. Everything was in the same state as they had last seen it, and the trees still looked as fresh as ever. Troye's eyes opened wide in shock as if he had seen the real world for the first time ever.

He followed Kyle as he directed him to walk through the woods and the glades. When he reached the glade, he found the pile of Becca's books on survival. It seemed like it was just yesterday when they were sitting there and having the time of their lives. In his mind, he could hear Jordan's giggles and Becca's playful taunts. How he wished to relive that moment once again! He wanted to rewind everything, but he did not have the option to do that.

Kyle knew he had to accept everything and move forward. After all, this was what life was all about. Kyle took a few steps, brushing off his thoughts about his friends until he reached the back of his house. He found that the ladder they had kept still resting against the wall. Everything showed that no one had come after them to look for them, and this was not at all surprising for Kyle. He never even expected anyone to care. He climbed up the ladder to the roof and entered his room. Troye looked around, fascinated like a child, at all the anime posters stuck on the walls. Kyle did not have the time to explain, so he rushed down the stairs into the living room.

"Mom!" he cried out. *"Anybody home?"*

There was no response.

Kyle figured by now that they had probably abducted his mother, too. They had to inform someone about this experiment, and they could not afford to waste more time. Troye and Kyle stepped out of the house, only to find the streets devoid of people. The trees rustled in the strong wind. The only sound that made the world look like a world of the living was the chirping of the birds.

Other than that, there was nothing. The absence of human life was eerie. They walked towards the road where a few vehicles passed, and he saw a female news reporter standing nearby recording the mysterious disappearance of the people of the city. Kyle and Troye knew what they had to do. They went to the reporters and told them that they knew what was going on. Kyle was panting while the news reporter kept the microphone in front of his mouth. He confessed everything without pausing for breath; he explained the whole incident and the great and cruel plan of establishing a new world order. He told them how there were so many people at the other end who were forced to suffer through this experiment and that, overall, this was not a very helpful idea. The news reporter was shocked and so were the viewers worldwide because the news was live on air. The two young boys had taken a very courageous, bold step.

In truth, Kyle and Troye were rebelling against the people in power – and that posed a threat to their lives. However, they did not bother about their personal well-being and only cared for the people who mattered to them. They knew that this step was essential if they wanted to release the people in bondage and so they had to put their own lives in danger. Maybe if people came to know about this, they would try to rebuild the real world together or find a new place to live and destroy the evil plan of the scientists. They needed to build a team and bring some clarity to others in the time of confusion.

Every person around the globe had one question on their minds: *"Where are our loved ones?"*

Everyone was worried because they had been separated from their families. Children were left abandoned as parents were taken into captivity. There was nothing good about this experiment, nothing good at all, and this was the truth that Kyle had exposed to the world.

Chapter 13 – The Battle Is Ours

The news of this barbaric act had finally spread all over the globe. Newspapers and magazines were printed and published at the speed of light. The people who were left behind were informed about the traumatic incidents taking place on the other side of the world. All this time, they had been in delusion; they were treated as puppets dancing at the command of the people in authority, with little knowledge of what was going on behind the scenes.

Not only had these people been used, but they had also been made into fools by being told what to do. They were stopped from thinking on their own. In this current situation, the financial elite, and the people in the government had the upper hand because the people carrying out the experiments did not involve them or their families. All of them were safe from terrible suffering and losses. These experiments were mostly being carried out in far-off places or on the outskirts of the town where only the poor and the helpless resided. As the lands where these atrocities were being committed were far away from the main centers, stories barely approached the main cities. Even the people who passed through, sadly, did not dare to talk about the horrors they may have seen. In this world, human life was expendable and replaceable, and all these people were numb to it. Even the truth was molded and displayed differently, and no one could recognize it for what it was. They had trusted the government blindly, but it was time for them to stand up for themselves, for their rights, and their identity.

The government was very craftily, manipulating them to follow what they had strategized, but they did not know the plan. They were not aware of the hidden hazards behind the innocent faces of the leaders. What they projected on media and how they pretended to be was not at all what they were like in truth. They came together with these scientists, and initially, they had planned to make this transformation to the world where they were living. They were misled and misdirected, but they had not known about it all this while.

The news circulating through the population took them all by storm. Kyle and Troye had not even expected this reaction from them, but they were glad they were able to talk about in public. Kyle had wanted to talk about narcissism in front of the people, and this situation had provided him with the platform he needed. Although narcissism was not exactly what he had spoken about, it did bring the idea to the fore and ignited curiosity in people to learn more about it. They wanted to know more about what was happening, and now that their people were involved, they had to wake up. This was a wakeup call for all of them who were going with the flow, who were allowing ill-treatment to take over them. Their love for their lost loved ones had made them think and contemplate about the life that they had been living so far. All this while, they had let narcissism take hold of them; they had let materialism shape their decisions and run their lives.

It was a world that prioritized material things and idolized money, but now they understood the value of human life and how fragile it was. It had made them connect with their emotions and go back to what the world was like before evil corrupted their minds and removed the empathy in their hearts. Kyle and Troye had not thought about the effects of expressing themselves to the public, but it was what they had desperately needed. They had to hear it because it was important for people to know the cruelty of the government. They were still young, even if they were doing great things, but they needed others to support them.

It reminded Kyle of the bible verse that his psychology teacher had taught him.

"Two are better than one because they have a good return for their labor: If either of them falls, one can help the other up, but *pity anyone who falls and has no one to help them up. Also, if two* lay *down together, they will keep warm. But how can one keep warm alone? Though one may be overpowered, two can defend themselves. A cord of three strands could not break easily."*

He could picture his teacher writing on the board and teaching them about the importance of teamwork. Kyle wished the people could understand this; it was not very hard to understand. People just needed to have empathy for each other and understand that no man was an island. Their lives were dependent on each other, and they could not win any battles of life all alone. It was an unchangeable fact that they needed one another especially now, in the case of this fight against the governing bodies, they had to unite to form a body too. They could either continue in ignorance or accept the wisdom and be conquerors. They had to work in unison and advance in the form of a troop.

Kyle, Jordan, and Becca had been renegades, and it was because of the collective effort that they had come to this point. Now that his friends were not there, Kyle was a little saddened, but he knew that ultimately they were going to experience their victory together. However, right now, the focus was on the leaders of the city who were misleading them. The people in authority knew everything, yet they were allowing the people to walk towards their destruction and bow down to cruelty.

On the other hand, the people of the city were confronted with a choice...the choice that they had been running from all this while. They needed to come face to face with this reality and had to choose between the worlds. This was also a choice between slavery and freedom, between love and hate, between truth and lie, and between their conscience and wrongdoing. No one understood that life never worked like that. How far could they run after all?

Life always had a unique way of bringing people back to what they had been running from; it never let anyone escape the situation that they were bound to face. In this city of vain dreamers, people had surrendered themselves to be slaves of the city leaders. They had allowed someone else to decide their fate for them and to alter the course of their lives, but now, when they are faced with the inevitable doom, they had to stand up and pick a side. They could not choose to ignore everything that was happening around them. This was a battle against their underlying stubbornness; a battle that was not letting them stand up. This was a fight against their dead consciences that had chained their minds to the thoughts which were similar to slaves, or as the people at the lab. Someone had to grab a knife and chop the chain away. Someone had to do it, and the universe had chosen Kyle for this job.

He was the appointed one for this great universal act of saving. In reality, even Kyle could not escape his vocation. No matter how disheartened he felt throughout his struggle with narcissism and bringing people to the realization of what was going on around them, in the end, he had to stand against the people and fight for the cause. Similarly, the people who were running away from the most significant choices in their lives were stopped. They had to look in the eyes of their fears and say what they wanted. Now was the time that they had to choose the leaders of the city or the conviction of their consciences.

Just like Kyle, they also had the threat of losing their lives because they could wipe them off in one go like the great flood of Noah. However, it was no longer about life and death, but about standing up for the right thing. If not today, they would never get the choice again. Kyle was extremely nervous, but now he sat back and watched because he felt like he had done his part. Now it was in the hands of the people to either allow themselves to be victims or to be in control of their own lives.

Kyle stood on the ground and glanced upwards at the vast expanse of the sky. He could watch birds flying freely with no one to catch them and keep them chained on the ground. They were free and enjoyed their liberty. He thought that the people of the city could enjoy this as well if only they had the wisdom to make the right choice at the right time. If only they could remove all fears, step out of their comfort zones, and step into the world that awaited them! They were entirely capable of building a beautiful world together, one without narcissism, materialism, and cruelty and where they did not even need any assistance of an experiment.

There was chaos all around; an uproar surfaced over the city like bellows of smoke after a war. The people began to walk out of their houses and started confessing who they supported. The choice had created a great divide between the populations. The people looked like the Israelites walking out of Egypt; it was like the parted sea where Moses stood on one side with the Israelites, while Pharaoh and his army were left behind.

The people could also either walk ahead and oppose the leaders of the city or stay behind and suffer. They could either bring about a change or go to the new world where they were going to be treated like captives forever. It was a tragic fact that there was no turning back in that case; they had to remain there for eternity. People were going through an internal war, and it was not even about the people anymore.

They were not helpless, and they had to realize that. Back at the lab, the forced patients had begun to regain consciousness. There was another room in the same lab which Kyle and Troye had not come across. In this room, there was Becca and Jordan who, very wisely, gathered everyone in one place. They searched through all the rooms in the lab, and they found the mirror which was located in the room on the top floor. These labs were in the basement, but the exit was located on the upper floor. The scientists and the psychologists who were involved in this had escaped the place, leaving these people behind, and now they could easily make their escape, too. Jordan and Becca led the people out of the mirror into the real world. They marched valiantly out the exit like the conquerors of the land. They were the ones who could turn the hearts of the rest of the people as they were the witnesses of the cruelty.

They could be the change makers by testifying against them and giving them a wakeup call. As they walked out, they had to pass by the forest, and because there was no path to cross the fence, all of them worked hard to break through it and enter the other side. It all seemed like a zombie apocalypse, but the only difference was that these people were more active than they could ever be, and they were going to wake up the sleepers in the real world.

They were going to tap their consciences awake. The people marched out through the city. They went far and wide, from house to house, speaking about what they had seen to anyone who would listen to them. It was more like they were evangelizing about a religion that they wanted everyone to follow, but they would also make it look like this religion was the epitome of truth. There was no truth beyond this religion that was being preached. Now, there were only two choices about the people they preach to: they could either renounce the religion, or they could follow it. Whatever choice they made, their eternal life depended on it.

Unfortunately, no one was spared, and everyone had to have a definite answer. They had to make a choice and not be like lukewarm water. They could not travel in two boats at a time because they were going to plunge straight into the water and suffer the consequences. They had to pick one side so that they could reach the shore that was waiting. No one was born to go with the flow, but they had to paddle on their own and take the turn wherever they wished to go.

Chapter 14 – Only You Can Find the Answer

It was like the apocalypse had arrived. People left their houses and advanced in herds, not caring about their valuables anymore. They feared for their lives and the lives of their loved ones. For a moment, material things mattered less than they ever had. Little children followed their parents, unaware of what was going on around them. There were loud noises of people enraged by the consequences of the experiments and the wrongdoings of the leaders of the city.

They shouted and burned cars and shops in protest. They demanded an answer which they were not getting. While there were others, who stood there mindlessly, walking in the stampede without knowing where they were heading. The children knew nothing of what was happening – they only trusted their parents. The saddest bit was that their future depended on the choices the parents were going to make. However, it was also good that they were not aware of the sad reality of the world. They were blind to it because their innocent minds could not comprehend it.

Their innocence was intact, and their mind had not been exposed to the evils of the world. They were the only ones who showed that there was hope for the generations to come. They could be the beacons of light in this dim, dark world, and the restorers of this devastated earth. But why did they have to suffer the consequences? Why didn't the parents have the wisdom to know that blindly running after any power or authority was only leading them to destruction? In this situation, they were the most helpless ones of all. It was the adults that were capable of deciding for themselves.

They did not have to rely on an external superpower to dictate them. They had to get up and rebel against the corrupt system and not let them continue with the old ill-treatment. The leaders began to send forces to abduct as many people as possible, but in such a way that nobody would find out. These people were mostly the ones who had not dared even step out the door. They had shut the windows and doors as if they could run away from the inevitable.

The forces caught them and hid them in the Labs that they had initially created before creating the other world. They had created small rooms under the buildings that belonged to the elite in the form of tunnels that made it hard to find them. It was a strategy that was unknown to everyone. So many of them had faith in this system that only sought its benefit. They were not going to consider the lives of the people if it did not assist them in any manner. All they had been doing was to gain fame, power, and dominion over the world.

If they were successfully going to establish this new world order, all the countries were going to be ruled by one government which was going to govern all the people like they were their puppets. The city of vain dreamers was going to extend throughout the globe. The whole world was going to be transformed into this strange world where even though there was going to be zero narcissism, and there was also going to be the loss of free will.

No one would be able to do anything other than obey; it was a place full of people, but they were just as free to move like the dead, lying in their graves. This process was carried on till days. The city leaders did not respond to the requests of the people who asked for an answer. The choice was given for many days to the people so that, among these days, they would choose the fate for themselves. The people camped outside and did not even return home.

This kind of rebellion was never seen before in history; the unity which people displayed in working for their cause was incredible. Even if they were foolish to stand up for the wrong side, they at least contributed their input in the whole situation. However, the people who did not wish to contribute were either taken secretly into captivity, or they remained inside willingly, thinking that they could not be any better.

These were the people who had accepted everything that what was happening was what they deserved. They were not even willing to change the circumstances, and this group of people was the most naive of them all. They knew what was wrong and what was right, but they had chosen to simply close their eyes and hope that everything would calm down on its own. They had gathered enough food and water to survive, and they did not have to step out in search of it for at least two to three weeks.

They were cowards only concerned about feeding themselves and their children, and not about what the circumstances could do to their lives. Their temporary bliss could lead to an eternity of helplessness, and they did not realize that they were putting their entire generation into the wrong hands. There was another group of people who were strongly against the government, and they decided to go to the wasteland. These people knew the consequences of being enslaved by a few top officials. Everything would be controlled at such a minuscule level that people would suffer due to poverty, starvation, and diseases. People at the higher levels, of course, would reap all the benefits.

People began to form their forces to defend themselves in case of an attack by the enemics. They had to live in harsh conditions, but the necessary provisions were made for them. Yet, they did not feel the deprivation because they understood the seriousness of the moment and were willing to face whatever came their way, without a trace of fear or cowardice. They collected all the weapons they could, whether they were just household knives or properly licensed guns that most of them had.

The rebellion had reached to the extent that they broke through the shops of ammunition and stole the weaponry for themselves. In addition to that, they decided to form their colony separated from the others. These colonies only contained the people who strongly opposed the leaders. They made plans collectively and were ready to fight at any moment. Kyle, Troye, Jordan, Becca, and Miley led this group of people like valiant soldiers preparing an army. They motivated them and encouraged them to recognize the dangers and stand up for the truth. They had all kept quiet for a very long time, but now they needed to fight in unison against the dark forces and overthrow the yokes of tyranny. Among the people who were abducted from their houses and were forced to be the subject of the experiments, they were also people who had not even escaped in the first place.

These were the ones who were transferred to the real world for experimental reasons and still suffered there. Some of them had died in the process as they were mutilated and could not bear the pain that was inflicted on them daily. Then there were some who, although alive, were barely clinging on to life. These tortured people were dumped on the floor, unconscious and with no one to help them out of their misery.

There was no hope for these people, at least not until someone would invade these labs and evacuate them; that, or the scientists themselves would release them from this undeserved punishment. Something had to give. However, until that happened, they were bound to suffer. The families who had not found these people either roamed in the streets or lived in the colonies waiting for justice to be provided and to finally see the faces of their loved ones after the chaos subsided. The loss was great, but they knew that their struggle was eventually going to yield to a better and brighter future. The days continued to pass and every day brought anticipation of justice and the final decision to be taken.

One thing was sure that there was going to be an end to this struggle they had been experiencing from so many days. The people had already taken the step that they should have taken years before. But this seemed like the right time when narcissism was at the pinnacle, and the government was exposed to everyone. The truth lay bare, and now, no one could claim that they were not told about the tyranny of the leaders.

No one could rise and ask for justice once again. This was the finale of the battle in their minds and the battle outside in the arena. The wrestling against injustice had begun, and they were either going to overthrow the government or let them rule and permit them to execute their plans. Kyle and his team wondered how there were still people who were in favor of the government. How could they possibly support these heartless, vicious rulers? However, the good part of this was that this group of people were a minority who wanted to be guided and guarded by the administrative rules. They liked the idea of having a governing body over them because they felt like they would be all over the place. What they failed to realize was that this governing body was slowly going to treat them as their slaves. They were going to be lab rats for the rest of their lives, and bear the results of their wrong decisions. Kyle personally thought that correcting them at this point was another foolish act.

If they were still supporting the leaders even after being well-aware of their behavior, it meant that correcting them would not make much of a difference. They had cast their lot with the government and would do what they had planned anyway. In this case, the best thing to do was to watch people make the decisions for themselves. The only people that had their sympathy were the kids whom Kyle tried to somehow come to the colonies so they could be safe from evil. Overall, these were the groups the world was now divided into and was set apart by the two sides. One supported the leaders because of their belief in the idea that they were capable of eradicating narcissism, while the second wanted to live freely, not being governed by someone else or being treated like captives when they were created to be free from all kinds of bondage in life. These were the ones who also respected the free will of the people but had sympathy for the ones who failed to make the right choice for themselves. No significant change came though they had all taken the paths that they wanted to. They had decided what they wanted and whom they wanted to support.

Kyle, Jordan, and Becca watched as spectators who had long waited to see this widespread transformation. They wanted the people to stop living lives of ignorance but come to terms with the truth. The next step was, of course, a matter of choice, but someone had to initiate it. Someone had to be the savior of these lost sheep.

The world that had long been a victim to the epidemic of narcissism now was divided into groups of people with different opinions. The choices they made reflected their thoughts and also told how perceptive they were. They showed how wise they were, and they had the fearlessness to combat against the direst circumstances. This was the time when the people were finally sifted like chaff from the grain – and it was not a forceful act but one that the people had willingly consented to. The people now had their rightful places, according to what was worthy to them. They still had the freedom to make their decisions. It was a free world as it had been all this while, although the freedom was also constrained to the will of the leaders.

They had only given as much leverage to the citizens as much as was harmless in their eyes. As soon as they thought someone would be a threat to them, they used to hush their voices so that even their screams would not be heard. Now, they could no longer do it, and everyone could enjoy the freedom of expression and speech as well.

Chapter 15 – Leave a Trace

It was a bloodless war. A revolutionary rebellion that conquered not just the bodies, but the minds as well. Even though the current state was in chaos, the aftermath was going to be the beginning of the establishment of proper law and order, or so they hoped. It was going to be a democratic world that would allow the people to pursue what they wanted to without being ruled by an evil force. The group of rebels was collectively working to bring down the mega-corporations who were internally corrupt. They were constructing this new world order that was eventually going to finish the concept of free will.

The people had realized the dire need of this, but they had always, in some way or another, been under the influence of the government. Their beliefs were shaped by what they were told since they were born. The corrupt system had also effectively corrupted the education system to manipulate the minds of the people from a young age. They were set up to fail to recognize the problems. They knew that if they planted the beliefs in the minds of the children while they were still young, and trained them the way they wanted to, it would be difficult for them to disbelieve and revolt against the authorities when they grew up. Therefore, in a way, the experiment had begun a long time ago. Everything was being orchestrated by the government quite meticulously, and corruption was intricately woven in the entire system, even though people could not see it. From the start, the educational institutes and media had projected the government as a body of leaders that sought the welfare of the people. They were portrayed as governing bodies doing great things to create a better world for them and the upcoming generations.

They were exhibited as trustworthy and reliable, upon whom the cities could easily depend on. Even the parents taught the same thing to their children because that had been ingrained in their minds, but now, it was hard to remove the thoughts from their minds. So, whatever values, customs, and beliefs they were taught as kids, they taught the same to the children. The children knew nothing about being free and having the liberty to make their own decisions. They did not know how it felt like when they could say what they wanted to say or worked what they wanted to work on and face no repercussions for their decisions.

Alas, there were terrible consequences for everything done by their own free will. Even the people who had grown up in the free world had forgotten their own opinions as they were accustomed to being directed by someone who had power and they were forcefully imposing this on their children as well. They wanted their children to succumb to the will of the leaders, and establish the world order the way they wanted. However, tired of the mindless following, these children who were persuaded to comply by the rules and regulations, collectively decided to leave their homes and set off to the wastelands where the colonies were located.

They hoped that their pleading would be heard over there and they would not have to bow down to something they did not support. They wanted freedom, support, and a place where they would have an individual identity and where they weren't replicas of other human beings. They detested the condition of the people who had fallen into the trap of the corporations. The entire world had turned into clones who carried the same thought processes and outlook towards life. These young minds did not want to be a part of the old order anymore; they wanted to bring an end to the mentality of surrendering to what the media told them.

They wanted to find out things for themselves and to not join the herd without knowing what lay ahead of them. They wished they could tell this to their parents or to their friends who didn't understand the major flaw in the government system and who were unaware of the consequences. Most of these children escaped because outright rebellion to the face of their parents would result in them being beaten or grounded at home. They escaped by climbing the walls late in the night so no one would catch them. They packed their bags with essentials such as a few articles of clothing, an extra pair of shoes, and first aid items.

These were the things that were going to be sufficient for them as they were embarking on this journey of survival. They did not even know what life was going to be like away from home, but it was surely going to be better than living under the rule of an evil superpower. They left everything behind and began living in those colonies, and even though they had to experience the struggle of starting a new life, they accepted it open-heartedly. All of them wanted to start anew, and this was the bravest thing that they could do. However, starting afresh by any means did not imply that they forgot everything that they had gone through.

They were not dumping their memories in the trash, so they would never have to face them again. This process of starting afresh was more than just that; it was not only going to be a transformation on a global level but also on the individual level. Their mindsets were going to improve. They were granted with an opportunity to change their future and to take things in their control. Now they could remove the hypocrisy and the self-centeredness that people harbored deep down their hearts. They could see that love for material things was utterly useless, and these things were not going to last forever.

The most important things in life were time, love, and care. Without these, life was a meaningless sprint; it would be incomplete and emotionless without love and care for other human beings. No one would have each other to support. As it was, very few people realized that life itself was the least loved of all. It was a precious gift that was bestowed to the most fortunate people, and every moment must be cherished with a thankful heart. It was not something to be trifled with and left to be gone to waste. While they had the chance to make the most of it, not taking a stand was the most foolish decision one could ever make.

It was time to realize the fragility and significance of life and how the lost time would not return. After many protests and questions raised by the people, the government leaders conducted a meeting that called their supporters to the east end of the earth. People packed their bags and set off in the already funded airplanes. The evil leaders tried their best to provide people with every need, so the luxuries of life could entice them that they were getting access to so easily. This was their last try to attract the people to themselves and combine again to fulfill their plans, and it was the last test for the citizens to either give in to their love for money, luxuries, and life's counterfeit joys.

They could once again give in to their carnal nature of being drawn to the material things. Or, they could be brave enough to fight the battle against their desires and recognize the vanity of these things. The people walked toward the horizon and slowly disappeared from the eyes of their loved ones. The end was finally here; the choices made seemed like they were never going to turn back now. They had bid the final farewell. The parents wished that their children would have joined them, but now they were at peace with the thought that at least they were making a choice on their own. Fountain Alley was left empty, and even the other world was empty. There was nobody there, so these rebels broke the mirrors and finished the gateway to this unreal world. They did not need one anymore because the earth had already been divided. On one side was the population of people with awakened consciences, while on the other were people who were willingly allowing someone else to rule over them. It was as if they had surrendered to fate without realizing that there was no such thing as fate. Everything that happened was the result of man's doing, whether good or bad.

Nothing was preordained or predestined because, if that was the case, it was extremely unfair. This is because while some people had good experiences, others had had bad ones. Therefore, it was essential to realize that everything was the result of their own choices, and everything was going to combine to decide the ultimate result. However, sadly, these people did not understand the power of choices and decisions. They only accepted whatever came their way even if it was all false and misleading. A strange and gloomy calm set over the cities as the sun dived into the sea, and the boats sailed off to their destinations.

The people's faces showed no signs of regret, although the kids missed their families and friends, and cried, thinking that there might have been a different way to do this. They began to think of all the alternatives that could have taken place, but everything was already said and done. There was no turning back; they had to accept their fates.

Children wondered, and so did Kyle, Jordan, and Becca, if they could still save their families. For Kyle, his mom chose to stay back with him while his dad took his sister and moved to the east end. He did not even say goodbye to Kyle, and that tore him apart. His mom was already used to his dad's ill-treatment, but she still wished for Mr. Williams to return to her and start afresh, not only as a father to their children but also as a husband to her.

In Jordan's case, both his parents left. Becca's case was no different, either. All in all, the two children paid the huge price of losing their parents, and now they longed to bring their parents back. As they watched other children unite with their families, they wished that they too could be blessed to experience the same. Tears oozed out of the corner of Jordan's eyes and then Becca starting weeping too. Kyle, who was trying to be strong through this entire time, gave in

CITY OF VAIN DREAMERS

as well. Tears trickled down their cheeks as they glanced towards the east. Was it all a dream? Was everything going to be restored? Their eyes were filled with hope. They wished they would meet again someday when life would not be so hard, and they would be capable of looking past their selfish ambitions.

Their intentions of meeting each other were true and pure, but the only question was: when would that day arrive? Sadly, no one knew when it would occur, and until then, this was the end of this long and hard struggle. It was a dead end ahead, and they had no choice but to accept the choices of their loved ones as well. They had to accept their fates and look forward to what the future awaited them in this new life free of narcissism and materialism.

They had so much more to do in life, and they could either dwell on their pasts or move ahead. Kyle, Becca, and Jordan were wise enough to move on and to use their hurt and loss to create something bigger and better. These little heroes had finally completed their mission, even though there was no particular conclusion that they had desired. However, one thing was made clear: no one was part of the unreal world anymore.

That world was a part of the past that was going to haunt them in their dreams forever. It was a reminder of all the lost souls who had surrendered to the cruelty of man and had not once thought to think wisely. It was also a reminder of how much they needed to value each other because life was unpredictable, and it was not necessary to always have a happy ending.

Sometimes life would leave you with an abrupt ending – an ending that left you with the uncertainty of what was going to happen next, and one that made you wonder, *'Is there even going to be anything beyond the end?'* Till then, there was only one last choice to be made: to accept the end or to find hope in that last moment of perplexity.

CITY OF VAIN DREAMERS

www.ingramcontent.com/pod-product-compliance
Lightning Source LLC
Chambersburg PA
CBHW021143090426
42740CB00008B/917